You Can't Kill "The Hoss"

Steven "Crazy Horse" Edwards

Copyright © 2020 by Steven "Crazy Horse" Edwards

All rights reserved. No part of this publication may be reproduced, distributed, or transmitted in any form or by any means, including photocopying, recording, or other electronic or mechanical methods, without the prior written permission of the publisher, except in the case of brief quotations embodied in critical reviews and certain other noncommercial uses permitted by copyright law. For permission requests, write to the publisher at the address below.

Liberation's Publishing
183 Cottrell St
West Point, MS. 39773
www.liberationspublishing.com

Ordering Information:
Quantity sales. Special discounts are available on quantity purchases by corporations, associations, and others. For details, contact the publisher at the address above. Or Call 1-800-325-8028
Orders by U.S. trade bookstores and wholesalers. Please contact Ingram

ISBN: 978-1-951300-87-6

You Can't Kill "The Hoss"

Steven "Crazy Horse" Edwards

Dedication

-This book is dedicated to my mom, who I love dearly-

Contents

Introduction 9
Chapter 1 11
Chapter 2 21
Chapter 3 27
Chapter 4 35
Chapter 5 41
Chapter 6 49
Chapter 7 65
Chapter 8 75
Chapter 9 81
Chapter 10 87
Chapter 11 101
Chapter 12 121
Chapter 13 139
Chapter 14 163
Chapter 15 177

Steven "Crazy Horse" Edwards

Introduction

I'm Steven W. Edwards, better known as "Crazy Horse." The name Steven W. Edwards may be one many people don't recognize. Most people don't know the man I am today. They just remember how I used to be. It is a good thing to know where a person comes from, but it's more important to know who they are in the present. God has a way of taking a person a long way.

"Crazy Horse" everybody wanted to know about him. He is one of the best friends a person could have. I take a lot, and seldomly get mad. I love the Lord with all my heart. That is how I am now, but in my past, I was just the opposite. I wasn't saved and didn't know right from wrong. What I did know I didn't care enough to do it. So, you want to know about me jumping off the bridge in Amory, MS? And almost killing myself. You want to know about my fights, my wrecks, and most sadly of all when I was taken from my mom at the age of ten?

It was me against the world, and it felt like God himself had turned his back on me. I have come to understand that it's not always someone else's fault.

It is about the choices you make. This brings me to the reason for writing this book. The books I wrote before this one does not include the details of my life. Here I share more details.

With no father or mother playing an active role in my life, I thank God I had loving grandparents. My mother worked to provide for us, and I love her. I had good examples along with the bad, but I chose to hang on to the bad. This made the street life mor appealing to me. I was rebellious. It was fun and adventurous, and I liked it. This is where the trouble began.

Some people may have thought I was a saint. You will soon realize I wasn't. Telling these stories about my life to show what God has done. I was the worst of the worst, so I thought. One day God stepped in and saved a worthless soul like me. Ever since I have been a changed man. Do I still fall? Yes, but Christ is so quick to pick me up. He did a work deep inside of me. He will and can do the same for you. It is God that has spared my life over and over and over. Now, you will see just how many ways "You Can't Kill the Hoss."

Chapter 1

A *Young Hoss*

I remember when I was about four or five. My mom and I moved back to Jackson, Ms. Because she was in love with Roger Denton Sr. At the time I didn't know he was my brother's dad, nor did I know I had a brother at that point. That is a story for another time. I remember like it was yesterday. My mom and Roger were working. I was with my grandparents until they got off. I was outside playing having a good time. I heard my grandad's voice, God bless his soul, say, "Stevie don't play around that hole I dug to put in those new pipes."

I guess he was working on a water line or something anyway that hole was deep, but do you think I listened? As soon as he turned his back I jumped across that hole. I made it across a good three or four times, but then I miss calculated my jump. Down into the deep hole I went. I was crying and falling in shock at the same time. I landed at the bottom of the hole.

On top of the world, my granddaddy was lost. "I turned around and he was gone," he told the others. I still hear him calling for me, "Stevie where are you boy come to granddaddy." I cried back out to him, "Granddaddy!" He found me. He looked in the hole where I was standing in the cold and dark. He yelled for Granny to call 911. She did and she also called my mom.

By the time mom got there, the fire chief was sending a rope down the hole to pull me up. When the rope came down, I grabbed it. They pulled me up and my mom was so happy, and so mad at the same time. I remember my mother was the first to grab me to see if I was okay. The policeman and the fire chief checked me out making sure I was okay. They couldn't believe I wasn't hurt. As soon as the fireman let me go, I ran into the woods. I ran into the woods and climbed up a tree.

Trees always made me feel safe. They were high up and no one could reach me. My grandad came looking for me. When he found me, he told me I wasn't in trouble, "Everything is okay." He said. I came down and the policeman and fireman checked me out again. I had no broken bones, "This kid is tough they said. The next day the hole was fixed. It was the only way my mom would let me stay. I thank God for my grandad may he rest in peace. If anyone is in heaven my grandad is. He is there waiting for me.

A Family Plan

I remember my mom came home and told me and Roger that she was pregnant. I didn't know how to feel at the time, but mom was happy. She told me that she wanted me to watch out for this baby. That made me happy. I think Roger was the happiest of all. He went out to celebrate and didn't come home all night. Oh boy was my mom mad. When he did come home, he told her he had gone to jail. She didn't believe him, because she had called every police station in the area looking for him.

Needless to say, he came up with a better lie and was let back in the house. Mom loved him, and we needed the money. That's when I knew I had to protect my sisters, but I didn't know how much trouble that would be. I know this is bad to say, but Roger was a terrible dad. He only thought about himself. He drank a lot, and only spent time with his family after having all of his fun.

When I was five, I remember thinking how happy I was with in life with just me and my mom in it. That was changing she fell in love with Roger. For a little while everything was ok. I don't know why, but I always had a feeling something wasn't right. We were a family and I had to make the best of it.

I remember when mom was pregnant with my

sister Carolyn. Roger was her father, and not long after he moved in. I was going to be a big brother. Mom was sick one day and needed to go to the doctors. Roger was nowhere to be found. Mom said, "Go to a neighbor's house and call for help." The police must have been in the area because they made it there quick. Thanks God it was false labor. She didn't have to go to the hospital. We still couldn't find Roger. We really didn't need Roger because I was there. A kid is still a kid though, and I learned at an early age I had to be a man.

Mom went to the neighbor's house to thank him. I learned that his name was Larry White. From then on, I called him Mr. Larry. I don't know if Mr. Larry is alive today or not, but he was a good man. He tried to help when he could. That is more than I can say for some.

I remember my sister crying because she was hungry, and I had to walk to the store to get something for us to eat. Like always as soon as I got back from the store there he was, and my God was he drunk. He was mad because mom had used his beer money on bills or food. It was the first time I saw him slap my mom. He did it in front of me and boy was I mad.

I went outside and got a stick. I came back in, and he was bending into the refrigerator to get a beer. I hit him in the back, and he fell to the ground. "Don't you every touch my mom again," I yelled at him. When He got up, I knew I was dead. Luckily, he was drunk and couldn't move fast. I went to check on my mom, and he kicked me in the back with his boots. I felt like my back had broken in two. Mom hit him with something made of glass, and by then the police came. Roger went to jail and mom and my sister were fine. Job well done!

Grandfather's Rage

Granddad found out about what happened. Mind you my grandad is two-hundred and fifty pounds and over six feet tall. He grabbed Roger by the throat with one hand and punched him with the other one. He held Roger's one-hundred and fifty pound body in the air as he demanded, "If you touch my daughter or grandson again, I will kill you, and no one would ever miss you!" Roger got his things and left. That would be the last time I saw him, so I thought.

My granddad let us stay with him for a couple of weeks until my mom got herself together. It was great to be home with him. I was able to climb trees and run. Wherever I went my sister Carolyn was right there trying to do everything I did.

One day I heard my granddad yelling at my mom. I ran inside the house to see what was going on. She said she was going back home to Roger. Neither me nor my granddad were happy with that. My granddad may have seemed mean to some, but to me he was the best. Without him I would not be the man I am here today.

A Dad Just in Time

Mom was sick and she was ready to go to the hospital to have my new sister. Roger was actually there this time. He took mom to deliver the baby. We loaded up the old rusty van that used to be brown before it got old. It would backfire and sounded like we were in a drive by shooting. It served its purpose and we got to the hospital for my new sister, Cindy Denton to be born.

We pulled into the hospital, in Jackson, Mississippi. We helped mom out of the car. She was huge and ready to burst at any time. Roger sent me ahead to get the nurse. I ran ahead to find a nurse, and as I was running, I tripped and fell. As soon as I hit the ground I tumbled on my head. It felt like my head and back were broke. I lied there thinking my mom was waiting on me to get a nurse, so I pulled myself up and went and found the nurse. Till this day I never told a soul about the me falling.

The hospital was full. Mom made it to the back. It seemed like for once roger was ready to be a real dad. He went to the back with my mom and told me to stay seated and watch my sister until our grandparents go there. He asked me if I was okay, which made me happy that he was considering me.

I told him I was.

I had to do something to pass the time. I put my sister in a wheelchair and rolled her down the hallway really fast. She was laughing so I went faster. For some reason I didn't notice the wet floor sign. I ran into the wet floor and the wheelchair spun out of control. It went flying and hit the wall, I went flying over the wheelchair and it fell on top of me. The doctor thought I was hurt, but I got up and my sister thank God had not been hurt. We went and sat down. By the time our grandparents got there we were the best kids ever. "Ya'll are some good kids," they said when they got there.

Back to the Farm

When mom took Roger back and dropped the charges that was the worse day of my life. He treated me one-hundred times worse. I remember we had a mean pit-bull and some other kind of crazy dog. He had gotten the second dog from off the side of the road somewhere. Every time I came out of the house those dogs would chase and try to bite me. I would always outrun them somehow. Roger thought it was funny.

Once my sister Carolyn was outside and the pit-bull ran after her. I ran and hit the dog over the head with a stick. The dog went down and when he did, I started to beat him. I almost killed that dog. Roger saved his life when he came outside and yelled at me to stop hitting it. I tried to tell him what happened, but before I knew it, I had hit the ground. He had hit me over the head with a stick. He told me to get inside. The dog ran for safety under the house, and after that I never had a problem with it.

Roger was drinking more and more each day, and the more he drank the worse he was to be around. He would use any excuse to leave the house after he started feeling good. That was okay, because I had already decided in my mind that I had to be the man and step up to the plate. Roger didn't mind. There were many times I didn't know what to do, but somehow, I found it out. I went on my path in life. I got it wrong a lot, but I realized that one day I would get it right. The only way to fail is the give up.

My Baby Sister Comes Home

I remember it was three days after we had taken mom to the hospital to deliver the baby, when they both came home, Cindy and mom. My sister Carolyn and I were at our grandparents' house. It was the best time ever, because I could climb trees as much as I wanted to. Time passed and I missed my mom. Grandad came and told us mom was coming home. My face lit up like it was Christmas Day. I ran and got Carolyn so we could get in Grandad's car. I literally had to drag her.

You Can't Kill the "Hoss"

My Grandad drove to Jackson, and all the way there my sister and I jumped up and down in the car. Once we arrived at our house in Jackson, I saw my mom and my new sister Cindy. Mom was sitting in a brand-new red rocking chair. It was a sight for sore eyes. I remember running over and hugging my mom and new sister. I remember mom saying, "this is your new sister Cindy and I'm going to take care of her no matter what.

Like always Grandma was in the kitchen cooking. I had forgotten she was there due to all of the excitement. One thing about her she loved cooking. He food was always so good; it was like eating out at a restaurant. We had fried chicken, mashed potatoes, and turnip greens. For dessert we had sweet potato pie. Oh, yea and let me not forget the best cornbread in the south as far as I knew.

Roger had to go to the store and buy milk, and had stay gone longer that he should have. I was glad he couldn't even mess up this day. It was a great day for everyone. I thanked God!

Steven "Crazy Horse" Edwards

Chapter 2

Back to the City

Everyone always wondered when my life took such a bad turn. I'm going to tell you it started when we went back to the inner city of Jackson, Mississippi. We moved in with Roger's brother Robert. He was slick. He could take your wallet and you would never know it was gone. He showed me how to go into a store and get what I needed without any money. He only showed me once and I must admit for the rest of my life I was hooked, (until I met God that is.)

Cindy was still a baby and my mom had to watch her close. Carolyn was running around playing, and Roger was working somewhere. He said he was working, but whenever mom looked for him, she would find him in the bar down the road. I was left to Robert and his vices. Roger loved doing crazy thing to you and whoever else was around.

I recall as driving as I'm driving back home to Okolona MS from my hometown Jackson MS today I'm taken back to some of the crazy times and crazy things and went to a lot of places that we did not have any business being and I thank God every day that I made it. This was a rough life at 11 years old but every time he would get some money, he would always give me some of the money and that kept my sisters feed, so I was good.

The Family Needs Help

Our family had one mouth that my mom and Roger had to feed, but they did the best they could, but my sister had to have diapers and getting sick and I think it was from being around all them chickens and dogs. As I sit my mind goes back to the good old days where it is just me and mom. I soon learned that everything in life will not go your way, and sometimes that is really your blessing in disguise. Roger and I was working in the chicken house until dark, and then we had to do the rest of the chores when we was done with that we had to house work, because my mom just got out of the hospital and couldn't really move unless doing house work.

There was this little church not far from our house and somehow, they found out we needed help. They brought us a lot of food and clothes, and I think they gave Roger some money. If they did, he never said anything to us. My mom made us go to the church, and I cut the church lawn in the summer. I was okay with anything to get me out of the chicken house. Roger would go and fix different things at the church, but I never saw him for a church service. He would say he was too tired or had too much to do. You would think a person would have one hour a week to spend with the Lord. If not, that might be a problem.

It came to the point that when it was time for

me to go to church Roger would get mad. "He can stay home and work. As bad as he is, he won't learn nothing anyway," he would say. Mom would take me to church anyway. When I got home, I had double the work. I had to make up the time I loss by going to church, was Roger's reasoning. "Nothing in life is free and you must work for what you want, so if you don't need to work today, then you didn't need to eat today." Even now when I recall those days sometimes, I start to cry, because no child ever deserves this kind of treatment. I thank you God for having my back.

Last Day with Mom

I was in Jackson and I had just gotten out of school. I had to hurry home because my sisters might be there alone, so I had to get home as quick as I could. When I got home both of my sisters was sitting crying because wanted their dad and they were hungry, and they were ready eat. Roger remember is my step dad but that was my sisters real dad anyway he was gone to the bar down the street just like all the Fridays before, but for the last month or so he did not go to the bar or nothing, and for the time he really started to act like a man and kind of like a father but anyway I think it was the welfare had been there about 6 weeks earlier because Roger left us home alone while he went to the bar but kid you not we was never in no danger, because first thing I would never open the door for anybody unless it was my family or the police this is what Roger said, so I heard a knock on the door and it was the police. When I open the door it was MS Ann as she kept calling herself every time she came calling herself being nice but she is the reason we got took from Mom it the first place I really hated this woman and the police for a while growing up because after that I thought all police was bad so usually after that if was going to get in trouble I would just run if I got in trouble but for me all the time in my life that did not turn out so great but that is story for another time and I don't want to spoil the ending so anyway back Roger and the Police and MS Ann, because for one we are there by our self-strike one and then no food in the house strike two even though Mother was going to the store to get food and I told them that but by the time Mom got back with the food and Roger got with the beer at least him only ran to the store and the beer this time so really if all this other stuff has not of happen really not would been said but anyway that was not the case this time we going to the with the state which sometimes know I should have went with the Mrs. Ann because at times I felt like the whole world and God Himself has turned their back on me but know I know better but at this in my whole is gone everything from birth till this point had just change but any way we went to my uncle's house which what we facing the look like the best thing so still I really wanted to be with but will be for another chapter but anyway my called my uncle Bobby and lovely wife Berinsine Edwards God rest her soul came to pick us in Jackson about 3 hours from I was staying but anyway it was what was best for my sisters because at this point I really care about to much but my sisters and my mom but for my I went with no problems

Steven "Crazy Horse" Edwards

Chapter 3

My New Home

Now we are in our new home in Pheba, Mississippi. It started off okay, but keep in mind I wanted to be with my sisters and protect them. This is where my dilemma lied. We were supposed to be going home for the weekends. After everything cooled down my mom was supposed to come and get us. As you already know that is not how things turn out. It would be ten years later that she would try to come see us. She tried, but our family kept up a lot of confusion. We had a big family. No offence to anyone, but I had my own family. I got into trouble a lot trying to get back to them. I wanted to be with my mother. My readers and family you must understand!

Okay, with that being said, I hope everyone that I did wrong accepts my deepest apology. I'm so sorry. I got most of it back. I harmed a lot of people who loved me so much. I felt if Mom could get to me, she would. So, I went along with the adoption. When signing the adoption papers is where the twist began. My mom's name was Edwards after my Granddad. At this time, he was my uncle. He later became my dad. He used to whip me really good. Looking back at it, I think he whipped me too much. I know I did a lot to make them hate me. They kept loving me anyway.

Learning from My New Family

My new family did what they could to make us to feel at home, but still I was still learning the rules of the house. For me it was pretty simple. Stay out of the way. If you don't work for your food, you don't eat. My Dad Bobby made sure that he had plenty for me to do. This is where I first found out the value of a dollar.

I know that this is bad to say, but we didn't know how to use a wash rag or soap and water. For the life of me I can't remember why it was so hard for us. Mother Edwards made sure that we learned really quick how to take care of ourselves. She did so much for this family keeping us together. Even though I didn't show it all the time, I loved her. I just had other things on my mind. I didn't care how other people felt.

We are in the heart of the bible belt, so going to church was going to happen. I promise I gave this woman so much hell for just trying to love me.

When I think about all the pain I caused. It really breaks my heart. Keep in mind that my heart was already broken. I didn't know how to love. Our Mom was a kind, small lady with a heart of gold. When you made her mad that changed. You had the whole house on you. When pops got home you got it again. Back in those days they whipped you with whatever they had in their hand. What does not kill you will make you stronger.

I would talk to mom a lot. Most times it was while we stayed up late and played checkers of some other board game. I remember once I got my butt whipped so bad could not sit down for a week. I had gotten into a fight at school. I remember mom sitting me down and asking what the problem was. She loved me very much. Sometimes we would sit and cry together. That meant the world to me.

I never told anybody that in my life until now. Like I said she was a good Mother, just not always. I was a good son, but at that point in my I couldn't trust too many people. At times, a would let my guard down and try to be a part of the family. It was a new family. I just had to learn the rules. They were pretty simple whatever Mom says goes and that was the law!

Good in School

When I was in school, I did not try my best, but somehow, I made good grades. Mom always made me do my homework. After we would watch woody woodpecker at three-thirty in the afternoon every day. After tv we would go to the garden and check it out. I had also had to feed the chickens and see if there were eggs in the hen house. I had done this before, so it was no big deal. I know now that the Lord made me smart to His word. Anything that came my way I tackled. I thought I knew more than the teachers. In my mind, I already knew everything because I did my work with no problems at all.

What I didn't get at school my Mom would always explain it to me at home. She made sure I got it even if they had to beat it into you! When you come to my house you better act right or you will get a beat down just like the rest of the kids. They did not play about anything. They were some of the best people you could ever meet, but they do not pay.

I can say I always did my schoolwork, because I sure did not want to stay home for some mess I got in! If you stayed at home at my house, you had to get up when it was time to go to school, and after you ate you had to go to the garden until dinner. Then, you came in and ate and right back to the garden until three-thirty in the afternoon. At three-thirty you went in to do your homework. Afterwards, you had to feed the chickens and work the garden until evening. Last you got your whipping and you got that whipping each day you were out of school. I guess I would be better off at school!

You Can't Kill the "Hoss"

Prove Myself

Every day It seemed like I had to prove myself. Sometimes it was hard to turn it off. I got in so much trouble for it. I always had to prove myself to everyone and that was almost every day. What I loved about it was, most of the time it always ended in a fight. That was okay with me! One day me and this boy Jason were going to race to see who was the fastest. We were to run to the swings and back. We took off! I jumped ahead of Jason and was gone. Jason started gaining on me and eventually passed me. Just like that I tripped him up. He fell and I won the race. Jason got up mad headed towards me ready to fight I was ready. I punched him in the face, and he grabbed me, and we were on the ground. He punched me and I punched him in the eye.

Eventually a teacher broke us up. I was in trouble again. I think everyone knows where I had to go, to the principal's office. This time it wasn't nice in the office because he was hot. This time they called my Mom up there and gave me three days at home. That was really bad. One thing the Principal told my mom got me into a lot of trouble. He said if it wasn't for Mary being a good student he would already have thrown me out of school. He also said if it happens again, I would be thrown out.

Mom was mad and couldn't get to her belt fast enough. She whipped me, but that was nothing compared to what my Dad did to me. When he got home, he whipped me with a belt so hard it broke the belt. I didn't even cry. I was so full of rage. I was fighting everyday anyway. When he hit me with that bull whip though. I couldn't do anything. Every time he hit me it tore my skin. I was bleeding so he stopped and told me to get up and go to the garden. At that point I was glad to get away. I thank God for everything He did in my life back then and now!

Time to go to Work

I remember pop was a hard working about five-foot nine real man. He worked at B & W in West Point. He would pick up hay for Mr. John right after work. I don't know how he had time to do anything else. On top of all of that he had a garden. I kid you not it was a mile long both ways and when I got there and that was my job and I hated it at first. When I would stop Ricky would always come and drop kick me in the back. I would fall flat of my face every time. I made sure I got to work. I thought I was tough, but I had nothing on Ricky. The harder I fought him back the more he liked it.

When I was not in school, I got up at daylight. When Mom got through cooking breakfast it was in the garden I went. That was where you could find me most of the time. I soon learned how to grow food pretty good. I remember the worst part of it was using that hoe. One day I had used the hoe all day. I cleared about twenty rows. I was tired. Ricky came and said keep working. I said I was done. Broke the hoe and that was the end of that.

When people say you don't know nothing, I didn't know nothing. My Dad and Ricky took what was left of that hoe and finished breaking it on me. The next day I got a hoe made of iron. They said now break this. My hands were sore, but I learned quick if you break something on purpose, you're going to pay one way or another. I learn my place at work quick.

It felt like I had a knife in my back. I had my two sisters, so I had to step up and be a man at twelve years old. I knew that something was not right when Ms. Ann said it would be awhile before my mom would  get her kids back. I overheard it. I had to act like I didn't because we had to get out there before we went with Ms. Ann. That would not have turned out good.

I love my Mom and all the people in my family, but I think they really put a knife in my real mom's back by not letting her see her kids. I know my real Mom made some bad choices in men. That cost her the true love of her life her kids. What can you do when you are in love? The word love is one powerful word. That is the reason it is used at will by anyone to someone you just met. That is where your problems will begin. Telling someone you just met, you love them to get something you want. I guess after that I always thought everything was a lie or a scam.

No one loved me, and that is what I gave people back in return. Most people that had a knife in their back would just lay there and die. I would take the knife out my back and put in the back who put in in mine. I keep going. I will not die. No matter what I will keep going on. That is one more example of how they can't kill the hoss.

Chapter 4

A Mother`s life is not always easy and fun,
but she knows these things must be done.
Mom how much I love your words cannot say.
You did so much for your family so we could make it from day to day.

I hope each Mother`s day is better than the one before,
because in my life I have not seen anyone that deserves this day more.
Mom there is so much I need to thank you for.
One thing I will thank you for having a Mother`s life,
and for making sure my life turns out right.
I know it was not easily to raise all these bad kids,
but when hard times came you never ran
or tried to hide and for that and a lot more
I say thank you and on this wonderful day,
I would like to say Happy Mother`s Day.
I love and may your soul rest in peace.

I know giving up her children was the worst thing my real Mom ever had to do. I always say you do not have a time machine; you can't go back and undo something that you have done. Once you've done something it is done. There are so many people that hold on to the past, so what if you used to drink and party. It's not where you come from, but where you are going.

The main thing to start with is to have God in your heart just like me. The main reason I wrote this book and the rest of my books was to let people know, if God could save me after all the things I have done, He can save anybody. It was not my Mother's fault that we got taken. It was Roger's, because if he had not been at the bar, or whatever he was doing this would have never happen. My Mother cried like a baby, and she was drinking after we got taken from her. It was a bad look for her, but every time she would just want the world to go away.

I love my Mom and will until the day I die. This is the lady that gave me life. It doesn't matter what happens I will always love my Mom. I see people are fixed too much on the past. I think if you have not done drugs in thirty-years it is safe to say that you no longer desire the feel or taste of it. My Mom is a good lady with a big

heart. In her past she got with some real bad dudes. It is sad to say, but they were not all that bright. The reason I say that is because they all did dumb things. They put the family at risk with his dumb choices. My Mother had to pay for her sins on earth. She lost her kids because of his mess. I just hope when I have kids, I hold them tight and let them know every day that I love them.

Going to School

I remember getting to school in hurry and get sign it. I had to meet new people and try to make new friends. When I got to school everyone was talking about Mary, and she was the greatest student in Cumberland. M brothers David and Bobby were great at tennis and in everything they put their minds to. Then there was me. Boy was U in for a big surprise. The first day of school was good until somebody tried to push me in back. As you already know, I pushed them back and it was on. After I hit the boy two of his buddies hit me from the back. I fell down and they started punching me in the head. S big boy name Zack came up and kick one of them off of me.

He throwed the other one about three feet into the air. The rest of them ran off. We have been friends ever since. I made another friend that day. I guess you couldn`t really call him a friend, but I did see him just about every day. He was in the principal's office and after he found out what happen he let me go. He said he knew my family, and that I would never be in a fight. I said, "thank you," even though I knew he was mistaken. That was my first and last time to get a free pass in school or in that office!

Adoption

I remember that it was time for us to go and make this adoption final. My sisters loved the idea. Mom didn't fight for us and for some reason she didn't show up. During the hearing, the only thing we did was sit down. The attorneys did most of talking. In my day kids did not speak to grown folks unless they ask you something. The Judge asked me if I loved these folks. I was older, so I got a say in the matter. I looked at how happy my sisters were. I was happy to see them happy. I remember, I signed this paper and then the judge said this is your new Mom and Dad. Everybody was happy!

We were on our way home and everyone was singing. We were in an 84'Ford truck and we stayed on the county line. We were on a gravel road. Six people were in the front of the cab of the truck. Me and my sisters were small so we didn't take up much room. So, we were coming down the road and we could almost see our house from where we were. All of a sudden Ricky came out our driveway in 76'Pontiac. He had just got it running. He used parts from the other cars in the yard. I helped him with the brakes and the steering.

You Can't Kill the "Hoss"

Anyway, he ran out of driveway at about forty miles per hour. He lost control, and before we knew it Ricky was on our side of the road. David hit the ditch, and it looked like Ricky just drove faster. They almost hit head on. There were parts of the truck and cars everywhere. I remember my Mom said, "God help us!" It was like the Lord had His hands on that truck because we walked away with no bad injuries. Mom hurt her knee, but both of my sisters were fine. Pop had a busted head, but the only thing Pop was worrying about was his wife.

The first thing out of his mouth was, "Mom you alright." She said she was fine, just her knee. He checked on everyone else. He got out of the truck, or what was left of it. Believe it or not Pop had just bought that truck two days ago. After he was finish checking on everybody he said, "Ricky you dumb S.O.B. You stupid jackass! Are you trying to kill us!" David was helping out Mom. I think he ran to the house and got the car.

Ricky tried explaining, "my brakes was out and steering gone." He was sorry and I'm pretty sure we went to hospital in another car. I didn't have one cut, and nothing happen to my sisters. I knew this was going to be fun because Ricky was crazy for real.

God's Hand on Me

I wanted to make sure everyone was fine and for some reason we felt like a family that day more than any other day that I could remember. My new Mom hurt her knee, but it was nothing like it could have been, but when you are under the power of God, nothing can touch you. Nothing in this world is more powerful than God, so that tells me that with God on your side nothing is impossible. My brother Ricky didn't get hurt either. I think he could run through a brick wall if he had to. That was how hard his head was. Ricky was not all bad just a little crazy. I guess a lot of him rubbed off on me. Most of the crazy things he did to me was to make me tough, and I liked it.

I remember Ricky would show me how to fight. The way he would kick me in the back of the head with his feet almost took my head off. I remember after I got up, he would kick my legs out from under me and then he would choke me out. Sometimes he would punch me in chest so hard it felt like he caved my chest in. It was going to take more than a wreck to take me out, because God has his hands on me. I want to say, "thank you God." for that because I would have been dead if it was not for you.

Chapter 5

That Go-Kart

When I lived in Pheba, MS. We stayed on a dirt road. For everyone that lived on that dirt road it was like being on the main highway in Jackson on a Friday. The county line club was about a mile down the road. I remember after they got full of beer, they would race down our road, my Mom called the cops on them two or three times. The cops got some of them, but the cops can't be on our road all the time. I remember one of my brothers got this go-kart and everyone at the house road it. I was the only one that could not drive. David took me for a ride, but I had to ride on the back. No driving for me.

My sister Mary was about eighteen or so at this time. She wanted to drive the go-kart. Everyone skipped her, so off she goes around the house. She was driving faster and faster. I looked up and saw Mary fly down our long rock driveway and going faster by the minute. About that time a car was coming down the road real fast. This fool was all over the road. Good thing Mary was able to stop the go-kart before going onto the road. The driver of that car must have been drunk or something because he drove on the wrong side of the road and lost control of his car and hit Mary and kept going. The car hit Mary so hard it knocked her and the go-kart over. To make matters worse the go-cart fell on top of Mary. We all thought she was dead. I heard someone yell for Mom and Dad to come outside. We all thought she was dead. I heard someone yell for Mom and Dad to come outside. We all ran to help Mary and by the Grace of God she was not dead. Thank you God He did it one time.

Hope She is Okay

My sister looked bad off when we first got to her. My brothers and I rolled the go-cart off of her. There was blood all over the place. David and Bobby tried to help her, but I think her leg was broken. She could not move. Mom called the ambulance, and everyone ran to Mary to comfort here while we waited.

I looked around for Ricky, and he was running trying to stop the car that hit Mary. The driver never stopped, he hit Mary and kept right own going like nothing happened. By the time the cops got there everything was already over. The driver was gone. Ricky told the cops that it was an older black man in a red car that had no tag number. Nothing was on the car and until this day I don`t think they ever found out who did it. The ambulance medical personnel got her up on the stretcher and in the ambulance. They rushed Mary to the hospital and most of the family went leaving Ricky and us kids.

That was fine with me. I didn't want to be at the hospital all night anyway. Ricky was mad, and we all loaded up to look for that red car. After an hour, my sisters started crying so we went back home. Ricky was still mad but at that point what can you do? Ricky got a call about ten that night. It was pop, and he said Mary had some broken bones, but she would be okay. That was the best news I heard all night. The cops looked for that car for a while but could not find it. I assumed whoever had that car must have hid it good.

My Big Day

It was my big day at school. I had a test and if I passed this last test, I would be going to the fifth grade. I was studying hard because I knew I had to pass. I got to school and found out that we would be testing all day. We only had two days left of school and I want to do anything wrong. I knew what was coming if I did. I sat down and went to work. Like I said earlier, I studied hard with my Mom. It was like she had the test in her hand. Everything we went over was on the test. My Mom was very smart, and a nice lady. Someone like me can get on anybody last nerves.

I passed all my test with flying colors and it was all because of my new Mom. When I got home and told her how I did she was so proud of me. This was another time I felt like I was part of my new family. The next day we didn't do much. I was so proud of myself because for the first time it felt like I really accomplished something. Trouble always seemed to find me thought. My friend Zack bet me I wouldn`t put a dead bird on this football players car. I couldn't resist. As I was going to get the bird Zack went and got the boy whose car it was. By the time I put the bird on car he saw me. That boy grabbed me and dumped me on my head. Then he took the bird and throwed it on me. That was nasty, but I learned not to mess with other people`s cars.

After my beat down and I had to go to the office. I told the principal that I was just playing, and he saw that I was already beat down, so he told me to go back to class. When I got home, I found out he had already called my Mother. She told me, "wait till your Dad gets home!" Those were the worst words I could ever hear. That meant a second beat down. Two in one day. It really didn`t matter I won me some money and made people laugh. Best of all I went to the 5th grade. In my life you have to look at the little things.

My Mother's Love

I know a lot of times I was hard to deal, but she never gave up on me. Believe me I tried, but for some reason she kept on loving me. That is what makes me still love her because she loved me. I loved her for that. For the ones reading this I know she has passed away, but I still love and miss her. I know she is with God and can still hear and see everything we do in life. My Mom stayed up all night when any of us kids was sick making sure we were okay. When one of us was sick Mom was the doctor. If you got into a fight with your brother, she was the lawyer and the judge all at time same time. I remember all Mom had to do to stop the madness was say, "I`m going to tell your Dad." That was it. Anyone who was not doing right got right and if not, Pop got there everyone better be right or Pop is going to get you right quick!

Tough Love

My Dad had tough love, and it helped me down the road. I worked with him hauling hay for Mr. John. Once we loaded about three-hundred bales of hay. We loaded it so quick so I could get paid. Pop went into the county line club and came out with a coke and candy bar and gave it to me. I took the candy bar and the coke because I was hungry. I ask Pop where my pay was. He said, "you eat at my table don`t you and what about the water bill or light bill." At that time, I didn`t care nothing about any of that. I didn`t have to pay them.

I thank my Mom and Dad every day that they didn`t give up on me. Most of all I thank GOD, because without HIM I would have been dead and in hell a long time ago. I thank GOD HE is not like us, running at the first sign of trouble.

My real Mom and my new Mom both used to

read me the bible just about every night. Sunday you had no choice You had to get the car and go to church. We went to a Pentecostal church, and they prayed the demons away from me. At that time in my life it seemed like I was running right for them. My favorite verse in the bible is John 3:16 "For GOD so loved the world that HE gave HIS only Begotten SON that whosoever that believe in HIM shall not perish but have EVERLASTING LIFE." (KJV)

I went to Church

My Mom would take us to church. With all I had going on church help. I really liked going to church, but it was like the more I tried to do good, the worse things seem to get. I now know that going to church had nothing to do with it. It was just the devil trying to keep me away from God and the blessings He had for my life.

My Mom was a real church going lady and she went right by the bible. She loved the Lord with all of her heart. My Dad did not go to church much, but he knew the bible too. My whole life I never heard of Pop ever drinking one beer. As far as I knew he never ordered one beer out of the county line road beer joint. I remember my Mom and Dad was married over fifty years before she died. That was amazing, because today if someone makes it five years, they are doing good. I think the reason for marriages ending is that they have taken God out of everything. When you think you are doing so good or doing too bad that you just don't need or have time for God, that is when you really need him the most.

I went to church and met other kids my age. For the first time no one talked about me. I really had fun at church. I knew the bible from front to back. It was fun for me to know the answers about the bible. I liked it when people called me smart. After that I read the bible more and more. Thank GOD! HIS words are inside my heart or there is no telling how I would have turned out.

Steven "Crazy Horse" Edwards

Chapter 6

The Big Fight

One day, Carolyn, Cindy and I are all getting on the bus. We are going to the back and this redheaded boy tripped Cindy. She had a bad leg and sometimes wore a brace on her leg. She hit the ground, and Carolyn jump on the dude. I helped Cindy up. After I found out that she was okay I went and took my book and hit the guy with it. That didn't hurt him because he got up and hit me in the mouth. I like it! The fight was on. I hit him in the head with my book again and Cindy kicked him. I think Carolyn hit him too.

I was tired so I grabbed him and opened the back door on the bus a throwed him out. The whole bus was yelling at the bus driver to stop. When he did, the boy was crying, and he had some blood on him. It wasn't a lot of blood, but I was off the bus for me two weeks. I got a beat down, but that was okay. I had to make sure my sister was okay. If I had to do it over again, I would throw him out the back again!

In Trouble Again

I got in so much trouble after that fight on the bus. I got put off the bus and Mom had to take me to school. My Mom was very busy during the day and to have to take me school put her behind. At that time, I did not really care. When I got home, I had to do my homework and then help Mom get done with what she had to do. Most of the time I just had to go to the garden and pick the corn, butterbeans, and anything else she wanted me to get. I did not mind, because I was eating good. When Pop got there, it was not so easy. It was time for the hay field for about two-hours. After that we came home and ate supper.

After supper, Mom would sit me down and try to talk to me. Everything she said I heard it. But when it came to my sisters all the rules went out of the window. People understand that about me. Yes, I did a lot of bad things, but sometimes I did them to protect my sisters. I was small in size, so I had to go hard every time just to survive. Guess what? That is how I liked it.

A New Day and Time

Once, I was in a town I knew nothing about. It knew nothing about me. I was trying to find my way around, so I went from the to the city to the country. It was like I was in the twilight zone. It got me away from Mrs. Ann and the police, so I was good. I didn't know anybody, except my family. I saw them maybe twice a year, usually during family reunions. I would get to see my grandparents, great-grandparents and cousins and my Mom. For a long time that was really the only people I knew at the reunion.

As time went on, I got to see certain ones more and more. I was so bad that no one could love me or so I thought. Now I know you must love yourself before you worry about what others think or feel. I think we worry too much about what other people think. I knew most people didn't like me anyway, so it really didn't matter what people said anyway. I thought, as bad as I was, they would have sent me back to my real Mother. Now I know they must have loved me more than I knew. I had to make the best of my life and the time I was away from my real mom. It was like I said it was a new day and new time for me.

My Real Mom Calls

I was outside playing one day, and Ricky said I had a phone call. This was a big shock to me because I never get phone calls. I get to the phone and my real Mom was on the other line. She wished me a happy birthday. She was a few days late, but it was still good to hear from her. I ask her what she had been up to. She told me not so much and that she missed us very much. She had started a catering business. She said she sent me a gift, but I never got it. I just always wondered why she didn't come get us or at least visit.

Nevertheless, she told me what was going on in her life. My Mom has always told me what was going on, but for some reason I was missing something in her voice. I could tell she was not telling me the truth about something. I was glad to just hear her voice. She wanted to talk to my sisters, so I called them to the phone. They talked for a while. Both of my sisters said Mom was coming to visit, but we never saw her. This is one reason my sisters didn't want to have too much to do with her even today. I know deep down they have love for her, but to keep from being hurt they hardened themselves. God can change anything or anybody heart.

All you have to do is to look at me and see at what he has did in my heart and my life! My real Mom said something to me that day that has stuck with me for the rest of my life. She said, "she loved me, and no matter what she loves me and never doubt that." I kept that in my heart all this time. That was the only thing that kept me going. I knew I would renew the bond I had with my real Mom. I thought of what I would say, or do when I saw my Mom again, but I most likely just tell her I love her and cry!

Prove Myself

Anyway, back to school life. We were getting ready to go to school and my sisters kept talking about this book fair. They had been asking for money for it starting the night before. I remember my Mom telling them no, so that was the end of it.

It was time for the bus to come, and we are starting to walk down the driveway. Carolyn showed me a wad of money that looked like about twenty dollars. I wouldn't tell on my sisters. She gave me some money too, so I would not tell on her. We went on to school. We had a good day. We were buying books, and games. I really forgot what all we bought, because we were buying books for kids that didn't have money.

We thought we were evening the playing field by trying to do something good. We had a good plan. If we got rid of the money, there would not be any evidence. Boy was we wrong. My sister Carolyn went into the office and tried to buy ten pencils. The secretary asked her where she got the money. She said that she got it from Mom. They called me to the office and asked me the same thing. Where did she get the money? I said that we got the money from Mom, so they called her.

Mom came up there and we knew we were in trouble. Mom was so mad because she couldn't get her money back. When we got home, we were in all kind of trouble. I tried to tell her I didn't steal her money, but she said either way it was my fault. I was the one who was supposed to be watching. I can't win for losing! My Mom got her belt and started hitting me. It didn't hurt because I was mad. No one was listening to me. I grabbed the belt and ran out the door. When I got outside, I was met by a blow. I didn't see Ricky. He kicked my feet out from under me. I was on ground. I quickly jumped up, I got up and I was ready to fight. I ran toward Ricky and he jumped in the air and kick me in the back of my head. I was out. He picked me up and knocked me down again. I think I might have gotten two punches in. Ricky was just too bad with them feet. I was so happy my Mom came and got Ricky off of me, because he was whipping me like I was a grown man. I took every lick! Anyway, my two sisters got a few licks. They were tired after whipping me. If I could do it over again I would. How much I love my family.

A Farm Boy

I was always working in the garden, and they would call me farm boy. I was not raised on no farm so why were they calling me a farm boy? I used to get mad, but I was in so much trouble already I really couldn't do anything. One more thing and I might get thrown out of school. I didn't want to do anything. This one boy named Jason came up to me and wanted to finish what we started earlier in the month. I told him, "no." I could not fight because I had too much on my mind. "beside I got beat really bad the last time I fought you so leave me alone." He knew something was wrong because of the look on my face. He went and told the teacher something was wrong with farm boy. I told the teacher that I was sick. They kept asking me questions. Jason raised my shirt and saw the stripes on my back. The teacher called the Principal and the Principal called my Mom. Mom called my Dad.

Mom came up there, and they sent me home with her. I didn't say one thing about nothing. When Pop got home, he whipped me again. It seemed like no matter which way I went it was a no win, no matter what! One thing about it, they never called me farm boy again. That hurt me worse than the whipping. Kids would remember that for as long as I went to that school. Once the other kids saw what I was going through most of them became my friend. Some of them still did not like me, but that was okay. Everybody in life won't like you. As long as God loves you. That is the Greatest love you will ever need!

Something I'm Good At

It was my second day and I had to wash the dishes after breakfast. We had the day off from school because of a teacher meeting. After we got through doing our chores, we were free for a while. We could do what we wanted. I went outside and there was a game room with a pool table and a dart board. It was a nice set up. I went inside the game room and got on the pool table. Robert and Kelly and the rest of the guys got a real surprise at how good I could shoot. I broke the balls and made a high ball from the start. Then I made about four in a row and missed one because I could not see my ball. Robert shot and missed, and it was game over. The rest of the games was much of the same it was something I was good at.

A *Brother's Love*

I recall once Ricky said he going to take me to the movies for my birthday. He had a Volkswagen® and the trunk was in the front. Before we got to the drive-in movie we stopped. I got in the trunk until we passed through the gate. Once we parked, I would get out of the trunk and could walk around. To listen to the movie, you had to stay in the car because the sound box was hooked on your window. Most of the people there did not care what movie was playing anyway. All I saw was a lot of people kissing. That was one reason I was walking around. Ricky had his lady kissing her and told me to take a walk. I could see what else I can see or do what I wanted to do.

I walked around and talked to some people, and we hung out for a little while. I went on to the next car, and there were some girls there about my age. I had just turned thirteen and you could not tell me nothing. I remember I got my first real kiss that night. I remember everyone at that car wished me a happy birthday. We left and even though I didn't get that girl's number it was one of the best days of my life. When I got home, my Mom had made me a big chocolate cake. We had a big meal just for me. Like they say, you never miss someone

 or what they did for you until they are gone. Mom if you can read this, I know you can because you are with Jesus. To you and Jesus I'm so sorry for all the pain I caused both of you. Saying I'm sorry is all I can do. Jesus I will always keep my heart with you where I will see my Mom again. God bless you.

It was my favorite time of the year, because we got to go to the family reunion

and see family members that I have not seen in a while. There were a lot of people that I did not even know. When we got to people, we did not know, our Mom would introduce all three of us at one time, and then we had to go play somewhere. That was okay. There was a lot going on and a lot of kids my age I could play with. It was great, but it still felt like some people there did not want me there.

They were mad at something I may have did in my past or mad at how I change what I did four years ago! People hated me for something I did in the past or future I'm really sorry. Like I just said I can't go back in the past. So, I hope you except my apology; forgive me; and live your life. I'm living mine.

I recall we were running around. At first David wanted to play tennis, so I tried playing. I was not very good, but I kept trying. That was not my sport, but when Bobby came on the court both of them would play for hours going back and forth. It was something to see. I still don't know who won it was always close.

I recall we were running around. At first David wanted to play tennis, so I tried playing. I was not very good, but I kept trying. That was not my sport, but when Bobby came on the court both of them would play for hours going back and forth. It was something to see. I still don't know who won it was always close. It's time to eat and there was so much food to eat. Mom made some chicken and mashed potatoes and cornbread. I think she even made a cake. All of that was small after we looked at what everyone else had on that table. I think we ate so much we couldn't move.

It came time to play softball and Pop was the pitcher for both teams. Me and David got on teams and that was plenty much it. All I had to do was to get on base and David would hit a home run or hit it over their heads and I could just walk home.

That was some of the best times that I had in a while, because everyone was running around playing baseball. Mom and her sisters and other family members were sitting and talking while everyone else was playing softball or tennis. My sisters were so happy, everyone loved them, and that was okay for me!

More Trouble in School

I had a bad day in school after I talked to my Mom on the phone after my birthday. I will not tell a lie I was crying because I missed her. I really didn't know what was going on with her, but anyway this was not the day to mess with me. I remember that it was recess and I was behind the bus crying. This boy came up to me and asked, "what are you crying for, do you need a bottle?" I told him to go on and leave me alone, but he kept on messing with me. I was already upset, so I punched him in his nose, and he started to bleed bad. I helped him get back to our class, and our teacher saw the blood and went crazy.

It was a little nosebleed, and if that dude would have got me down, he would have done me worse. The way I look at it we are even! This teacher grabbed me and hit me in the back with her paddle. I lost my mind or what was left of it. Before I knew it, I grabbed the paddle and threw it. Then I picked up a desk and threw it at the wall and ran out of the class. As I ran out, I noticed that the whole class was in shock. I was in more trouble this time than ever. I remember they had to call the police to come get me. I was hiding in the field house. They heard the wrong story. They said I went off the teacher got hit by the desk. The only thing that saved me was that I did have a bruise mark on my back.

I had to go to a psychiatrist before I could return to school. When I got home, I tried to explain my side of the story. It did not do any good, because I guess the desk must have bounced off the wall and hit the teacher. It got me the beaten of my life. First off, I hit a woman and then hit her with a desk. Secondly the police were called to the school. All I was doing at first was crying about my Mom. It did not take long for people to know if I'm crying leave me alone!

I can't believe it. I did go see the psychiatrist. Everyone at school saw me throw the desk at the wall and it hit the teacher. At this point no one wanted to mess with me. I think I went too far for Pop. He was so sick of all this and I guess I could say so was I. As much as I was tired of getting in trouble, I still would love to have fun when I was not at home. There was always work to be done, but I was still a kid. I wanted to have fun, but that was enough of getting in trouble. I started doing things and blaming it on someone else. I don't know if you can really call it blaming them when you leave the evidence in their locker for the teacher to find.

I remember it was about a week since I got in trouble and like I said things are good because other people are getting in trouble for my stuff and I loved it! I could go home and do my work or whatever and not be in trouble and everyone was bragging on how good I was doing. If they only knew they would have a fit. I will take the good times however I can get them. My Mom was so proud of me, but I had that hustle in me. These kids were way slower in life than me. I showed some of them how to shoot dice for money. Of course, and I showed them my rules. When you play by my rules most of the time you were going to lose. If you won, it was because I let you. Even still it was good to be good for a while.

Found the Football Field

I was getting into so much trouble that the principal said, "why don`t you try out for football?" I went and talked to the coach and coach said first I had to be the water boy. That was okay because I was part of a team. It wasn't long before the coach changed his mind. He said, "I like your spunk." He let me practice. It didn`t matter how hard they hit me. Believe me they were trying to kill me, but I got right up. The coach liked that, so he gave someone else the water boy job.

I was playing for Cumberland bulldogs and I was ready too. The coach put me on defense, and I had the right side. I would shoot the gap; I would tear a quarterback apart. Every time I was on that field, I gave one hundred percent on every play. I recall we caught an interception. The boy who caught the ball running was trying to score. The other team's fullback came running at him, but I got there first and knocked him out with one lick. That boy was seeing stars all night. Our runner walked in the end zone for the score and the win!

The one thing about that game or any other game not one person came and watched me play. They would always drop me off and pick me up afterwards. That was okay. It gave me time to do something without them anyway. This was what I needed to channel some of that negative energy. By the time I got home, it was time to go to bed. There was not too much trouble going on. Except for some fights, that was every day. What else was new? My two brothers Bobby and David tried to teach me tennis, but I could not beat them. I tried hard every time though.

I remember Bobby Jr. playing basketball, and when he got ready to go to the hole, he would throw elbows and score. David shot from three-point land or take it to hole. He was 6`2 and about two-hundred-twenty pounds and 30 years old. He was hard to handle. Sometimes David would go the hole all by himself. I would blindside him and steal the ball. He would get mad and tells me if I foul him again, I was going to get it. That would make me say come on with it! He would take me to the hole, and I would foul him, and he still scored.

Then he would say, "Boy you can't hold me, so stay out my way." It was like it was just me and him giving it our all. I loved that, and like I said before, that is the reason I'm so tough today!

Steven "Crazy Horse" Edwards

Chapter 7

Ricky Working on Cars

My brother Bobby hired Ricky to work on some heads on a car. Bobby was a mechanic, and he knew my brother Ricky needed a job. He hired him for two-hundred and fifty dollars. That was perfect for Bobby, he was busy and did not have the time. Bobby Jr said that was all the car needed. It would be ready to go, and this car was fast like all the rest. When Bobby Jr got home, he went to check on his car. Ricky said he could not get the heads off, so he got a jack and put it under the motor. He jacked up the motor and that would make the heads pop off. During all the commotion, the jack broke something on the motor, and that motor was done.

I heard Bobby was mad, but the only thing he could do was buy another motor. Ricky was already paid, so he got off free as a bird. The only person Bobby Jr. was really mad at was himself for letting Ricky work on it in the first place. Bobby Jr. and David was always working on cars; racing them; or testing them out for the weekend. I don't know why Ricky could not get it together when it came to fixing cars. He will keep trying if you keep paying him. I liked how he did things. He would keep trying until he got it right or made it worse. Either way he never gave up.

A Broken Lamp

I remember I had been good for two weeks, and for once our house was going well. Thank God! I was tired of getting in trouble, so I made sure that I did not get into any fights or anything. I was even making better grades in school. I woke up, and my Mom was cooking breakfast. She cooked pancakes and eggs and bacon the best breakfast ever. I thought this was going to be the best day ever. My sisters woke up in a bad mood from the start. Cindy got one of Carolyn's shirts and it was on. Mom made Cindy take off the shirt, so nobody got to wear it. My Mom finally got that under control, and we went to school. Everything that day was fine until we got off the bus.

My sisters were still fighting about that shirt. This time Carolyn pulled Cindy's hair. Cindy hit her, and it was on. I finally broke them apart, before we got to our house. Thank God! It was about a half a mile up the driveway, so I had time to break the fight up. When we got to the house, they were still yelling at each other. Mom asked, "what happen?" They were trying to explain, and still yelling. Mom said that was it, and she went to get the belt. I was heading to the door, but before I could get out the door, Cindy pushed Carolyn and she fell back into a lamp and broke it.

I could remember thinking how glad I was it was not me, because my Mom just got that lamp at Christmas. It was one of them that had the glass touch that had the shape of diamond hanging down off it. Even though the diamonds were fake it still was nice. My Mother loved it. You could imagine how much trouble my sisters are in. I ran and tried to separate them. Mom went and got the belt and started hitting them. They finally stopped and Mom said, "Wait until your dad gets home. You two are in big trouble."

I helped clean up the glass, and my sisters were crying. I knew they were in some big trouble. I had to help them out, so I went outside and got a brick and threw it. It broke the car window out of Mom's car. I did it just for my sisters, and my mom told my sisters to go to the back yard and play. All the trouble was on me from that point on. It was for a good cause, so I guess it was worth it.

I think when I broke that car window I went way too far. Mom was so mad at me she forgot about my sisters and that lamp. She called my Dad from work and told him I broke his car window. As you can imagine he was hot. he got home that whipping was worse than anyone I had ever had before it was really bad. I think I got beat with everything that Ricky and Pop could fine, and then I got whipped again with that bullwhip and every time it hit my skin it would cut me wide open and there was nothing I could about it. I remember Mom trying to talk to me, but I would not tell her why I did it, all I could say was I don't know. To make things worse my Mom and Pop had enough of me so much they called the police and the police said send him away he is nothing but trouble, but first let's send him to Psychiatrist and him what he has to say. I went and seen the Psychiatrist and he ask me was I happy and I said not really and then the man said ok, so in my mind that meant I was finally going back to my real mom but how wrong was I. I going to get sent to Independence MS it was a boys and girls Christian home to tell you the truth a different place for me to live might do everyone someone some good. I told everyone goodbye at school and then we all got up one Saturday morning and headed out and Pop had a 84 ford pickup truck with a camper on it and that is where me and my sisters had to ride. I told my sisters don't worry about me that I will be okay and that I loved them and for them to be good. I remember when we got there Mom and Pop got out went to the office and sign some papers and we looked around and Mom told me she loved me and that was that and now I'm at my new home for a while but it does not seem so bad.

Independence Day

I was in Independence, Mississippi, at the Mississippi Sheriff's Boys and Girl ranch, and I had to say it was not as bad as I thought. I was now away from everyone I knew. I can adapt to anything or anywhere. I would be quiet to see what was going on and then I would open a little bit but only what I wanted to tell them. I had the nicest house parents you could ever met, and they let you know the rules of the house right from the start. The rules were not hard to forget because they were posted on the refrigerator with your name beside it. A list of the chores you had to do for that day and for the week. It was okay because whatever chores I had to do was nothing like I did at home. So, I was good. My house parent's names where Mr., and Mrs. Smith and like I said they were nice and tried to help me fit in as much as they could. You have to think there were eleven other boys in the house with problems of their own. It was my Independence Day, because I was free from all the pain and bad things that I was going through.

Learning More About God

Every day before we ate breakfast we had to pray

and learned one verse in the bible. This was before we could do anything else. that was okay because I loved reading the bible. I learned that God loves me no matter what, and even when you mess up, he is still there. It did not take long for me to make friends because most of the kids had the same problems as me. It was easy for the kids to relate. I even got to talk to the head of the program and I could tell him whatever was going on in my life and he would try to help but I really didn't tell him much because I really don't trust to many people. I think the man's name was Mr. Dan and think he was a minister because he was always the one to talk to the kids when they had a problem or just needed to talk. Mr. Dan said he sees my record and he was not going to judge me based on that and made me feel good because for the first time in a while someone gave me chance and didn't assume I was bad from the start. I saw that day that God had his hands on me, and Mr. Dan showed me the power of God if you will let Him in your heart.

Fitting in

Sometimes it was hard for me to fit in because I always wanted things my way. I soon found out that you can't always get your way and if you get mad no one really cares. I knew I was in a nice place, because no one was talking about hitting. My house parents had only one rule of the house and with that living there should have been simple. Except the one rule was to follow the rules on the refrigerator. There was a whole list of rules by your name, but still it was not a mile-long garden.

My first week I had to wash dishes and that was not so bad because I have washed dishes plenty of times but it didn't matter what the job was I would get it done. There were two boys in each room and my roommate's name was Robert Frost. He was crazy. He was always talking about hurting himself and being in space. I was crazy too, so I fit right in. We would talk, and he would tell me he didn't like this one. He would say that you and I tried to tell him these people was not that bad. I think too many had done him wrong. I told him that these people were not like me. I think he really didn't care what I said, because he was bad about cutting up at night. I guess he was having bad dream because he would wake up in a cold sweat yelling at the top of his lungs. It would wake everyone up. Because of his craziness no one paid too much attention to me and that was great.

Can't Go to Sleep

We had to have the lights out and in bed by nine at night on the weekdays and eleven on the weekend. That was not too bad, but sometimes you just couldn't go to sleep. It wasn't always my fault. My roommate Robert Frost would not shut up. He kept us all awake. Mr. Smith would come in the room and he was mad. Once he told us to come with him, and I knew I was in big trouble. We went and got a bucket, a toothbrush, and soap and we had to clean the floor for about an hour.

I remember cleaning about half of the floor, while Robert really didn't do that much. He just sat and talked about space, and how he didn't want to be there. Mr. Smith came out and saw me taking a break and told to hurry up and don't let Robert do all the work. He let Robert go to bed and I had to stay up and clean the rest of the floor and Robert was the one that got us in this mess in the first place. The one not working but I'm the one that caught that seems to be the story of my life.

I was so mad but did not say a thing and then about ten that night, he came and ask me was I ready to go to sleep. I said yes and I went to my room. Robert was pretending like he was asleep. He heard Mr. Smith's voice. I was so tried all I could do was to go to sleep. Mr. Smith had the nerves to say, "Be quiet and go to sleep, Robert is sleeping." I just said, "Yes sir!" and went to sleep.

The Next Day

I remember the next day was Sunday. I had cleaned the floor till ten o'clock the night before. I overslept and got in trouble again. I was new, so they let me make it. I was mad and went looking for Robert. When I found him, I told him if he keeps setting me in trouble, we were going to be fighting.

He thought I was playing, so he just laughed it off. From then on, I was watching him.

Anyway, I was the last person to get ready for church because I had to wash the dishes and take a shower. I made church just on time because the church was in the next building. I got a blessing out going to church because the preacher told me about Jesus. He told me it didn't matter what I had done. God can forgive both of us. It was the first time I felt good about myself. I went to the altar to pray and to see if God could help me.

I got on my knees and started to pray. The preacher came over and said, "let it out son." I cried out like I was a baby. I could feel God`s Spirit come over me. I got up and felt like a new kid. I didn`t know how to use what I was feeling on the inside. I did know from that on, GOD was with me.

Steven "Crazy Horse" Edwards

Chapter 8

Time to Play

When we got through with our chores we got to go play or do whatever we wanted. I went walking around to meet the other kids on campus. It was the first time I had some free time to just chill out and do nothing. I went to play basketball and that is where I met everyone else. There was one the guy named was Kelly. He was about six feet and sixteen years old. He could dunk a ball without trying hard. It seems he was the cool type everyone wanted to hang out with him.

We finally got to meet the girls, and some of them looked good. I saw Kelly talking to this girl. She was about 16 years old with long black hair. She was so sexy and came over and started to talk to me. She asks if I had ever been with a lady. I said no, and she touched my arm. I got a little excited, and all I could do was sit there.

Laugh if you want, at the time it was not funny, because my whole face was red, and I really could not say anything. I sat there for about two-minutes and I got up. I went in the house, but they talked about me for about a week. That was okay. What they were saying really was not that bad. Besides, everyone got to know who I was all at once.

Made Some Friends

I was in a new town and had to learn to fit in with new people I knew nothing about. So far things were going well. I made friends at that place quick. Most of these kids had the same problems as me. I still thought I was funny, and they could not help but to laugh. Most people did not know this about me, but I would do some dumb things to keep people from laughing at me. I know what you are thinking, how are you doing all this dumb stuff. Be the class clown and don't want people to laugh at you? I did not want people to laugh at me because of how I dressed or how poor I was. Laughing at how I talked would make me so mad that I would be ready to fight.

I would make people laugh at what I was doing and not so much at how I dressed or talked and for me that was a hard way to live. Being a clown took me a long way. Kelly came to me and ask me if I was mad, and that he was just playing with me. He had a friend that he wanted me to meet. Her name was Rebecca Davis. I had seen her earlier that day. I really didn't know anything about her. Kelly said she was alright, and I guess I was going to have to take his word for it.

Going to the Movies

The one thing I liked about this boy's home was that they gave you an allowance, and they would take us to the movies. The boys and girl got to ride on the same bus. I got on the bus and Rebecca

Davis was on the bus. She even saved me a seat beside her on the bus. We got to talk the whole ride there. The first thing she said was how she thought I was funny and made her laugh. She said she had not laughed in a while, because she got in trouble and her mom and dad just dropped her off. I don't think she had forgiven them yet. I could see the pain in her eyes when she talked about her mom and dad, so maybe for one night she could smile and have a good time.

We were so caught up in each other I really could not remember what the movie was about or really cared. On the ride home I held her hand the whole way. Later on, I got me a kiss. I was on top of the world, and no one could bring me down. When we got home, I walked her to her room. I could have gotten in big trouble. I walked her home anyway to show her I didn't care about the rules. My heart was beating, and I was scared as a sinner going to church. I knew what would happen if I got caught. I didn't let Rebecca see none of that. All she saw was Mr. Smooth. Before the night was over, I got many more kisses and then climb through my window and went to bed. I must say that was one good night.

I Think I'm in Love

That was the best night of my life, and I could not sleep that good. All I could think about was Rebecca and getting to see her again. The next day was Sunday, and I could not wait till I got to church. I would get to see Rebecca. I know that should not be the only reason I wanted to go to church, but I was young and in love. When I got there, I saw Rebecca, and told her to meet me behind the church in two-minutes. I went and told Mr. Smith that I had to use the bathroom and he let me. And said, "Hurry Back!"

I went behind the church, and there she was. She was about six feet with long brown hair. She had on a sexy red dress. My heart could not take it, and as soon as I saw her, I ran up and kissed her. We talked for a minute and then we went back inside. I could not tell you what the preacher talked about that day. All I knew was I was in love. I was taking a lot of chances just to be with her. I really, I don`t think I cared too much about the rules, because as much as I tried, I just could not do right. It made me think was any right in me.

This was a good day because for the first time I had a girlfriend and was going to church learning more about God and his love for me. On top of that I was making good grades in school. I was smart in school when I sat down and tried. Most times I wanted to be the class clown just because I wanted to fit in. It seems like I could not do no wrong on this day, because for once everything just felt right.

When I got back to boys' home everything was

great too because it was report card day; mine was great. I remember that all good report cards got extra money on report card day. and I had 3 B's and 2 A's so I had some good money coming to me. It was 5 dollars for every A and 3 dollars for every B. Then my girlfriend came over and gave me a kiss. Also, I got to stay up late. This was the best day of all.

Went to Office

I was outside just talking to the boys and not messing with anyone. Mr. Dan called me to his office and told me to sit down; he wanted to talk to me. I sat down. As soon as sat down I ask him, "What did I do?" He said nothing he just wanted to see how I was doing. He also said how I was doing really good by following the rules, really good. It was like I always said, "what he don`t know won't hurt him." I was glad he thought I was a saint. Then he told me my family was coming to visit me. My face just lit up because I was going to get to see my family. Mr. Dan told me to keep up the good work. Then told me go back to my room.

Steven "Crazy Horse" Edwards

Chapter 9

My Family Comes to Visit

My family came to visit me, and I was so happy to see my sisters, mom, and dad. We got to have a picnic and we laughed and had a good time. I think my Mom and Dad thought I would be begging them to go back home, but I was happy. It was a great day for me and my family and everyone got to meet each other's family. I got to spend most of the time with my sisters and that was great. The most important thing in my life was my sisters and my real Mom. At that time that was all I knew. It was getting dark and my family had to go back home. I told them that I loved them and then they drove off. I still had to go and help clean up, and after that I went to slept.

Time for Camp

It was time for camp, and everyone got up early. They could have caught the bus, but like I said the early bird gets the worm. If you didn't get on first, you would have to sit on a seat with a hole in it. Sometimes the metal in the seat would tear your clothes, and that is never fun. We had to go about one-hundred miles to camp. All the kids were so pumped up. We had a whole week of light chores and lots of fun.

We could just relax and be a kid. The camp

leader had a list of everyone's names and where we were from. He also told us what rooms we were in. It was just my luck. I got the room with Robert Frost. If you recall Robert was my roommate at the home. I guess whoever was your roommate at the home was your roommate at camp. That seemed like a good idea. Robert was kind of crazy and I was trying to get away from him. But what can you do?

I liked the first day. We sat around the campfire and ate marshmallows, told ghost stories, and then after that we all stood up and prayed and went to bed.

Robert Goes Off

The next day Robert was still mad because the camp called the home. He was in trouble. The whole day he was mad. We all got up and went on a hike. For some reason Robert did not stay in the group. It was not long before the staff found out he was gone. Some of the staff went to find him, and they were mad. I knew where he was, so we went and found him. That was more trouble for Robert. I'm not going to lie. At first, I was laughing, but after I seen how much trouble he was in I felt really bad.

I'm the one who broke into the concession stand in the first place. No one on the staff saw anyone break in, but Robert had all the candy and chips in his bed. It was really dirty, but they would have blamed me for sure. They finally got him calmed down, but it was too late. He was already headed back home and did not know it yet. The staff sent Robert back to camp while the rest of us kept on the trail. One of the staff took him back to camp and made sure he was in his room. About thirty-minutes later Robert destroyed the entire room.

We had to come off of the trail when the staff found Robert. He was mad and was in no mood to be messed with. The staff was trying to talk to him, but Robert was not having none of that. I heard Robert say that if people don't stop messing with him something bad was going to happen to them. My God why did he say that, because when he did, they called the police. The police talked to everyone. they took Robert to jail.

After the police had taken him away the rest of the day went great. We had a lot of fun. We finished our hike and then we went camping deep into the woods. I remember being in the woods and walking right over a snake. I liked to use the bathroom on myself. As fast as the snake appeared it slithered away in like three seconds. After that I watched where I walked. The next day we got up and cleaned everything up and started everything all over again.

The Last Day of Camp

It was our last day at camp and everyone just wanted to do their own thing. The staff let everybody do what they wanted, and everyone went wild. I remember I went hiking with some of my friends, and afterwards we went swimming. Later the staff called everyone inside for lunch. This boy named Brad dared me to put some mud on one of the camper's sandwich and you know me I did it. I grabbed this boy name Jerry's sandwich while he was in the bathroom and put dirt and mud on it and then put everything back on the sandwich and then put it back on his plate. When he sat down and took a bite and his face turned another color and he spit it out of his mouth and he threw up all over the place and everyone laughed and because Jerry loved pulling pranks all we could do is laugh. I made 5 dollars on that prank and the bad thing for Jerry he is one of the ones that helped pay me, but the bad thing for him he went to the bathroom and everyone else had already sat down and I wanted that 5 dollars real bad. The rest of the day was most of the same everyone pulling pranks on each other.

Time to Go to Bed

I remember it was about seven in the evening, and I knew I had made it without getting pranked. Boy was I wrong because Jerry got me good. Jerry told me that someone on the staff wanted me because I had a phone call and when I walked toward the office Jerry threw water on me and one of the other guys throwed dirt on me, I looked like some kind of mess and everyone laughed and after that one of the staff took the water hose and clean my off. I was still dirty so they made me go jump in the creek to get clean but that was not so bad because I knew their time was coming. I had to put that aside because I had to break into the snack machine again. This time we were not playing because it was the last day and there was nothing the staff could do anyway, but I don't think they cared anyway.

We just went crazy on that camp that night and no one even cared to stop us. It was about two in the morning and everyone else was getting in bed but not me, I had some payback I still had to dish out. I came in the room and Jerry was asleep. I got some glue and glued his hands together; then glued them both to his head. I went and got Brad because he was the one who threw mud on me. I took his pillow and glued it to his head. The rest of the guys I took a marker and drew all over. Then I went to bed because I was tired. I woke up late and when I looked in the mirror someone had drawn on me too. Boy! That was one great week.

Back from Camp

We made it back from camp and everyone was so happy and so hyped up we never even sat down because as soon we got there we had to unpack and then get ready to go to town because it was movies.

Everyday there was always something to do and that was good for me because it kept me out of trouble so the more, I had to do the happier I was.

Chapter 10

Mom Talks About Cancer

Me and my Mother was sitting around talking and she told me that she used to have cancer, but she survived. I asked her what happen, and this is what she said. She was pregnant and had cancer at the same time. She had some women cancer down below, so the Dr said that it was best if they just get rid of the baby. It would not be born right, but Mom still didn't want to do it. Roger went and signed the Doctor's papers to get rid of the baby and that was that.

This had to be rough, because they had to take her cancer out at the same time. They caught the cancer just time, and it was not that bad. Thank God. It goes to show you, if God has his hands on you, there is nothing you cannot overcome.

Going Back Home

Everything in my life at this time is going well, but like always as soon as something good happens there was sure to be 100 bad things waiting to happen to me. In my life that was how it goes but at this point in my life I was ready for anything. I got called to the office and again I knew I was in trouble, but Mr. Dan said go pack your things you are going home. I just stood there and could not believe what I just heard, because I just made new friends and just passed 6th grade everything was going good for once. I really could not say anything anyway because what I said really didn't matter anyway but if I dared to say anything when Pop talked because I knew what I would get so I shut my mouth and done as I was told. It was the next day Pop and Mom and my sisters came and got me and just like I came to that home I left just as quickly. I got a day and a half to spend with my girl before I had to go home. I remember we spend every second we could together and I even climbed up my window and went and set under tree and kissed and talked to her for almost all night and told her that everything would be alright.

Most you think Rebecca was worrying about us not being together anymore but that was just part of it because her bigger fear was that I was going back to the same thing I just came from because this girl really loved me and I'm not going to lie I really loved her too. I told her everything would be alright and not to worry but about the time it got light Pop was there and just like that I was gone and did not get to tell her goodbye

Starting Back Over

My Dad said he could not afford to keep me in the because it was 50 dollars a month and I still had to come home and boy was I mad and I said to myself that this was the last straw. My Mom said we was going to start over but all I could think about

You Can't Kill the "Hoss"

was Rebecca and I would never see her again, but I guess I should be used to it by now. I love my family but at this point in my life I felt like they just messed my life but what can do? I tell you what I done I got mean as hell and the way Pop was, we were sure to bump heads. I remember me and Barbara's kids went in the woods and was playing hide in go seek and we had bb guns, so you better hide good or be able to run fast.

The good thing for me I could hide good and run fast but I was not fast enough because Robert and Kevin came from behind a tree and Kevin shot me in the back. I ran as fast I could and now Danny and Ricky got involved but I didn't care because I had a plan. I ran and got under the house and everyone ran back to the woods to get me because they thought I was in the woods for sure, and when I was sure everyone was gone back in the woods I came out from under the house and got on top of it with my gun. I sat on top of the house and waited for them to come back but they never did, so I yelled out where they could hear me, but Robert saw me and told the rest of the kids. I still was able to get a shot on

Danny I think I hit him in the arm but while I'm shooting at Danny both of his brother's was shooting at me so got behind the chimney and that was working for a minute but because I was behind the chimney I could not get a good shot on anyone.

I got tired of being pinned down so came out in the open so I could get a good shot on someone but Ricky came out of nowhere and shot me in the back and in the leg and knocked me off the house. I was alright but I fell right in the flower bed and when my Mom came out and saw me in her flowers she was mad and Pop came off and whipped me being on top of the house and for tearing up the flowers and by that time everyone else was gone just my luck. Well I told you that I was starting over again.

Getting My Payback

I got a good whipping after I got shot off the house and I was mad that no one else got in trouble but me. I had a plan to get even but I had to be quick so I waited until no one was watching and I put super glue in the bottom of their shoes and Robert put on his shoes he felt something sticky and pulled his foot out. To tell you the truth Robert messed up everything because Danny and Kevin never put on their shoes because they knew something was up. I did not know it but Jennifer that was Barbara daughter saw when I put the glue in the shoe and told on me. Once again, I got the beat down of my life so where I stand I could not win for losing but one thing I told God right then was if I ever have kids I going to make sure that they never got done the way I was. I don't want you to think the reason I telling you is for you to feel sorry for me because that is not at all the reason I'm telling you or writing this book or just about the money. The reason I write these books is to lead people to Christ and to tell people if GOD can save me HE can save anybody and maybe if I share my life story with the world maybe some of the mistakes I made someone else might not make. I will be the first to say I made a lot of mistakes, but I paid for them all and then some but keep reading this and see if I can get my payback.

Wonder Women in the Cornflakes

Me and Carolyn and Cindy had been playing super hero and I the Incredible hulk and Carolyn was Wonder women and I can't remember if Cindy was any of the super heroes but we played super heroes all day and that we got to watch the cartoon the next day because it was Saturday. My Mom fixed us some cornflakes and we had to eat them on the patio me and Cindy was already eating and Carolyn came out on patio spinning around and yelling something about Wonder women and kept spinning around and lost her balance and I tried to catch her but she still hit the table and landed in the cornflakes. I remember cornflakes and milk all over me and the floor and when Mom came on the patio and saw what happen all she could do was laugh and told her to clean up the mess but from that day on I will never forget Wonder women in the cornflakes. I will tell everyone beside the Lord and my Mom my sisters are the most important people in my life and I need to spend way more time with them now that we are older because people let me tell your family is the most important thing you can have in life.

The Fun Is Over

I recall wanted to go play with Barbara kids but today I had to work in the garden and then after that I had to help my Mom plant new flowers but I really didn't mind because I got spend time with my Mom. There was always one thing that I could always count on was that garden it had to be worked. I was in the garden and I was in there for about 4 hours and I was tried and it was so hot and I was the only one in the garden so I was going to take a break. I stood up on my hoe taking me a break and out of nowhere something hit me in the back and knocked me on my face. When I got up it was Ricky had throwed a huge dirt clough at me for not working and it was on.

I was so mad I ran right at him but before I could get close to him, he jumped in the air and kicked me in the back on the head and then he jumped on top on me and he beat my ass like I stole something. I told him this was not over and later on that night when everyone went to sleep I jumped on top of Ricky and I was beating the hell out of him until he woke up and relived what was going on. We woke the whole house because we were fighting all over the house and for the first

Ricky was bleeding too and he was at least 12 years older than me a grown man fighting a punk kid but Ricky found out that like so many that I was no punk I will let things go for a long but in the end I will get you.

We Both Want Some More

Ricky didn't like what happen to him because his lip is busted and I knocked a tooth out of his mouth, but like I said he was tough and you would almost have to kill him to make him quit. When Mom and Pop got through whipping me, I was madder than when I jumped on Ricky and when I get like that you really don't need to be around me. I remember while I was getting whipped Ricky was steady running that mouth, I can still hear him now, boy I hope you don't think this is over because I got something for you, and I told him if he ever put his hands on me again I would kill him.

I got another whipping for saying that but no one said nothing about what he said but that was okay because I told him what I thought and didn't care about the licks on my back, and really to tell you the truth I kind of liked it. I used my pain for fuel to get back at Ricky for getting me into this in the first place but I guess I'm in a lot of mess now because Ricky is not going to like me. I told that he better not go to sleep again so Pop locked me in another room just so everyone could get some sleep because I got beat down so much Pop was tired and

Ricky so even though I was bleeding Ricky was bleeding too and got a tooth knocked out so all and all I had a good night.

I'm Ready to Fight

I stayed up all night thinking what I was going to do to Ricky if he ever put his hands on me again and the things I was thinking about doing was not nice because I had enough of getting beat everyday by Ricky just because he could. We knew Mom and dad was going to the auction every Friday night and Carolyn and Cindy went with Mom, but I said I was staying with Ricky because I didn`t feel good. I was ready for the biggest fight of my life but just as everyone was about to leave my brother David came up with his wife Juanita and they wanted me go hang out with them because David did not like how Ricky treating me. David was not the big brother but when he spoke for some reason Ricky did what he said and just like I went home with David and had the best time of my life.

A Day with David

I remember David let me do what I wanted so for the first in some years I didn`t get beat and I just got to be a kid. We got to play basketball and we even played some tennis and then Juanita`s sisters and brothers came over and we had fun playing hide and go seek and time to chill without all that mess. Juanita was so mad about what was happening to me that she wanted to go and cut up right then, but David told to let it go for now and if things get worse, he would do something. I told Juanita at the time she was my sister in-law that I was used to it and not to worry about it because I knew if she said something I would get beat down even worse, so really, I just her to be quiet but I knew she was going to say something. I had fun playing with her brother and sister`s and she had a lot there Barbara she was the book worm type going up and was smart, and then you had Linda she was the one that never played by rules and she very out spoken and could fight and run with all the boys.

Then there was Doris she always quiet unless you made her mad then look out, but Doris was just smart and could tell you about anything because Doris love to read, but whatever Doris said that what went. Juanita had 3 brothers', first there was George, and he was more like me he did what he wanted to after a week with me. The next brother was Terry and Terry was a little fellow and he was tough to be little he used to follow me and George around. Finally, there was Albert, and he could take a computer apart and put it together, I know he could spend a whole day just messing with computers. They all were good kids and we all got alone good I had fun hanging out with them all day.

They Went Too Far

When I got home from hanging out with David my brother Ricky was mad because he said he had to do my chores while I was gone, and I had to go right to garden. Juanita saw Ricky and she let him know what she thought about what he was doing to me. Ricky went on about how bad I was, and no one wanted me and if she was so worried about how I was raised they could keep me, but as soon as David came out of the house Ricky shut up. David told Ricky don`t put his hands on me again and David got in his car and drove off. I wish that they would have kept their mouth shut because what happen next like to have killed me.

Ricky came up and grabbed me and we he did it was on because as soon as he put his hands on me I hit him in the nuts and I know you was told never to hit below the belt but I was tired of Ricky putting his hands on me. I recall I picked up a stick and soon as I pulled to hit in the back of the head, but Pop came out and took stick and beat me with it. Ricky kicked me in the head and knocked me to the ground and he beat the hell out of me and all I could do was just lie there and take it because it felt like my ribs was broke and again I told Ricky don`t go to sleep and he hit me in the mouth and knocked me back down and told me to shut the hell up. I told Ricky that was the last straw and this was not over.

Tim For Me to Go

    I was up all night with my ribs hurting and boy I was mad as hell and I was going to make someone pay. I always heard before you make a big diction in your life you need to pray. I wrote on a piece of paper God help me and keep me from doing anything wrong and all at once I heard the Lord say bust out the window and run away, so that night I put a rag around my hand and broke the window and went to sleep. The next morning, I wrote up early and waited for Pop to go to work and I crawled out the window with a black bag and then I went to get my bike but my Mom heard all that noise and looked out of the window to see what was going on and as soon as she saw me she asked where I was going and I said I was gone.

The next thing she said was leave that bike here, I said fine and I took off walking and I was walking with a purpose because I was ready to get out of there and then I started running like an inmate escaping from prison. I recall every time I saw a car; I would throw my bag in the woods so no one would think anything was wrong. I got a break a saw someone that did not know me and was going to Maben the same place I was going to call my brother David so I think that man may have been sent by God. The man asked me what was going on and I said nothing I'm just going to live with my brother, so he took me to piggy wiggly in Maben and dropped me off. When I was growing up everyone was listed in the phone book or you could call the operator and get the number that was because everyone had a house phones and now no one has house phones and everyone has cell phones, boy how time has changed things that back did not seem even possible. I got to the phone and called my brother David and ask him if he could come and pick me up at Piggy wiggly in Maben and David said just stay there.

I looked up and there was the sheriff coming right for me and I went to the phone acting like I am making a call but he was having none of that and he came right up to me and ask me my name and then took me home and the beating I got that day was worse than what I got for breaking the window because this time the law was involved so what I did in their eyes was real bad. I did not care how many beating they gave me I was going to leave there no matter what.

David and Juanita Save the Day

I knew that David was coming but I really didn't know how it was going to turn out but one thing for sure it could not get any worse. I remember Ricky jumped on me for not working but my ribs felt like they were broke and my shoulder was out of place and I had a black eye and a busted lip so no I did not feel too much like working, so when Ricky jumped on me this time there was nothing I could do time but lay there and take it. As I was laying there bleeding I saw David and Juanita coming up the driveway as Ricky was still kicking me and every time he hit me or kicked me it felt like I had a glass mirror in my belly because every time I got hit it felt like glass was breaking inside me I was in a lot of pain.

When David got out of car Ricky grabbed a big knife but for some reason David kept walking toward Ricky and David told Ricky to put that knife down before he took it. I stood still to see which one was going to win and David told me to go get in the car and that is what I did. I saw Ricky put that knife down and then disappear in the woods and that blew my mine because I never saw Ricky back down from anything but I saw it today and Ricky was supposed to be big brother. David and Juanita went in and talked to Mom and Dad and after I said my goodbyes I was gone to Okolona and I never had to live there again.

Steven "Crazy Horse" Edwards

Chapter 11

Moving to Okolona

I made it to Okolona and the good thing was Juanita family stayed right beside us in the next traitor, so there was plenty of kids to play with. I had so much fun even David got out there and played basketball with us and at that time I was about 13 or 14 years old and David was about 26 or 27 years old and I thought he was old. We got started playing and David was just going to the hole when he wanted to, and I was glad he was on my team because with David on my side I could not lose in life or while we were on the same team. We were ready to play football and me and George was on teams against David and Terry was a little thing but big at heart, but we still lost because no one could tackle David. I told George the plan if David caught the ball again, we were both going to hit him and knock him out and make him drop the ball that is easy enough. Terry hiked the ball and threw a short pass to David and he was running toward me and George and at the last second David saw what was going to happen and moved out of the way just in time because me and George was coming wide open but we missed hitting David and we hit each other and we was out for a minute but after we caught our breathe we was back ready to play but to matters worse David scored a touchdown and won the game with that play but all and all I had a good time. Thank you God for sending David and Juanita to get me out of that hell and when I say out of that hell just means, it was a place where I did not want to be because hell can be a lot of things for so many if it is something you don't want to do or some place you don't want to be, but for now my first day in Okolona was great thank God.

Juanita and David Lays Down the Rules

Juanita told me she didn't want none of that nonsense I use to and things were going to be different and I'm all for a new start but somehow your past will always catch up with you. I had to been in the house by 5pm on the weekdays and 10pm on the weekdays alone as I did good, but like I said, I don't think there was no good in me because that was what I was told so I didn't have much to try for. I think for the first time Juanita and David cared about me as a person and this was something that I was not used to.

David said he would do what he could for me all I had to do was to ask him. Juanita was the rough one of the two because she was not going for any kind of crazy mess and she would let you know, but I love Juanita like she was my real mom because when my life was at its worse she and David was there and that means more to me than you will ever know thank you both. I had my own rules, you make your rules, and I will try to keep them but I couldn't I would try very hard not to let you see what I was doing. I thought this was going to be a piece of cake but Juanita had her eyes on me but that was okay because at least she paid me some attention good or bad but I have to say living with Juanita and David was the best thing that happen to me.

Day Two at Okolona

I been in Okolona for 2 days and so far I was just feeling my way around to see what was going on, so I decided to take me a walk and as I came out my driveway I heard some loud music down the street so I walked down the street to see what was going on. I walked down the street and this boy was on the porch playing heavy metal music very loud and came up and ask him his name and he said Donnie and from that day we were friends for life. I went inside the house and met his Mom, and her name was Marie Parish and this lady was like my real Mom because she didn't even know me and let me come in her house like I was one of her kids. I was having more fun in 2 days than I had since I was at that camp and boy it felt good to just be a kid again. I didn't have to work in no more chicken houses or a mile long field or haul any hay, but the hay part I did not mine so much, I was just glad that I was not getting beat so I was good thank you God.

My Life is Good

I hung out with my brother David and had so much fun and for once everything in my life was going well. I went back down to Donnie's house and I met his Dad but when I saw him I knew he was Mr. Wayne from the auction, he was my Mom and Dad's friend and then I remembered Miss Marie and the reason I did not remember her at first was she worked in the kitchen she was always making money doing something. She was the kind of person that would give you her last dollar if she knew you really needed it, but Wayne would try to hold on to it but like always the women always win. Every time I would come over, she would always feed me and about 6 or 7 more boys that did not stay there but she did not mine. The next brother my age was Daniel now was not slow because he was smarter than most, but he looked like he was slow and that is how he got you every time. I did not know it at first but these 2 could help me scam this whole town because they did not know me. I know that was the wrong way to think but when you grew up the way I did that is the only life you know.

Getting Ready for School

Juanita and David took me up to the school and signed me up because they were my legal garden and I had to go to school. The school took one look at my record and shook their head and really didn`t want me in the school but they have no choice right now. My first day at school everyone was trying to fine me out and I was trying to get a feel of the school and the people in it. Every class I had to ask someone where the next class, so it was getting time for lunch and went to wash my hands and this black dude came up to me and said hey white boy give me your money and I said hell no if want my money you come and take it and the fight was on. I found out later on the boy's name was Terry Moore and he was nothing to play with.

Now back to the fight, Terry tried to hit me and missed and I hit him in the jaw and he just took that and hit me it jaw and when he did I took a step back and tripped his feet and he hit the ground and I choked him out and took his money and he had 5 dollars and all I had was 1 from the start so I was a winner even way. Later on, that day Terry came to me and said I did him wrong, but like I told him, he was going to rob me first so the way I look at it we were even.

Time for me to Play

My first day at school was not bad I met some friends and won a fight and I got 5 dollars so to me that was a good day. I got to school, and all the kids talked about was me robbing Terry, but I told them he tried to rob me first and everyone that he stole money from knew I was telling the truth. It was getting close to dinner, so I went to wash my hands and Terry and some more guys were shooting dice and Terry ask me if I knew how to play and I said no how do play. I said no that I have never heard of the game but that was a lie my uncle Robert showed me ever card trick and dice game that was ever made and then he showed me how to cheat so this should be good.

We got to shooting dice and I was asking questions like I did not know what was going on and when Terry felt relaxed, I took all his money and the money he took off the other 2. Terry was a bad loser and he wanted round 2 so there we went he would hit me and I hit we was beating the hell out of each other until we heard Coach Ford was coming and everybody got away but me, because they told him it was the new white boy but they was not sure who I was fighting. I remember trying to run out of the bathroom and ran right into Coach Ford and ask me what happen and who I fighting with, I told him I didn't know who it was and everything was fine. He said boy you got heart and anybody with that much heart and energy needs to play football and I need to meet him on the football field after school. I hurried up and got back to class and everyone knew not only was I tough and could give and take a beaten they didn't know I had plenty of practice, and they also knew I was not a snitch and has always went a long way in my life good or bad.

Beat Down of My Life

I thought that I was home free when I fought Terry but I did not know that Coach Ford told the Principle and he called Juanita and she called David and I was scared because I knew I had a beat down coming. When I got home, Juanita ask me why I was fighting and I said some boys tried to rob me so I had to defend myself, and she was mad but she just said tell it to David. I was thinking of the worse because everyone else sent me away so why not them to, but to my surprise when David got home and told him what happen and told me not do it again and to be careful I was shocked and almost past out. Now Juanita was not so nice but that was just with her mouth but when said something you she meant business, but beside my real mom of all the places I had ever been I love living with her and David the most.

I know I was bad and I'm real sorry for all the hell I put you and David through, but please believe me everything I did was not on purpose, but when cheating people and stealing and conning people is all you knew since you was a baby, I'm sorry to say but when the chips are down you will do what you know how to do to survive. I knew that day they really loved me and from that day on I had their back too. The reason I say that if someone thinks about messing with Juanita or David you going have to fight me first, because you have heard of ride or die, well in my eyes that is what David did for me. Ricky was his real brother but David still was ready to kill Ricky if hit again and for that I got David and Juanita back wrong or right and there is not many that I will have their back if they are wrong, but I love these 2 with all my heart and just saying I'm sorry or thank you does not let you know how grateful for you 2 for getting me out that mess and for not beating me yourself.

A Friend After All

I told myself that I had 2 fights in 3 days and something has to change, so I told myself that today I was going to do right if that was even possible because I don't know if any right was in me. I think I was a magnet for trouble because everywhere I went trouble was not too far behind, or was it me this whole time? Juanita let me have it before I went to school, she didn't hit me but she let me know what was going happen in school. Number 1 sit down shut up and number 2 no fighting no matter what but sometimes that was easier said than done when you got someone in your face ready to hit you in your mouth. The 3rd rule was don't let me get a call from that school or that is it, so now I got my rules I was ready for school. I got to school and everything was fine until after lunch when I went to use the bathroom and these 2 boys that lost their money the day before shooting dice and they wanted to win their money back but I said not today because I was already in enough trouble.

Then they got tough talking about taking something and one of the boys pushed me I pushed him and the other boy came out of nowhere and knocked me down, he hit me like I owed him some money and both of the guys went to work on me it was real bad. I remember seeing one of the boys get punched by Terry, I don`t know where Terry came from but I`m so glad he was here. After Terry punched the one boy then he hit the other one too and when I got on my feet I put the boots to them and that I is what I was doing when Coach Ford came and saw me, but it was okay because I just made a friend for life.

Crazy Horse Is Born

I got to school, and it was like I was famous because again everyone was talking about me and how I took what them boys gave me and then gave them that much worse. I had people coming up to me and asking me to do all kinds of crazy things and then they would bet me money I would not do it. The first thing I bet on was could I drink a bottle of hot sauce and I did it, and next bet was I had to drink whatever the boys mixed up and was nasty because someone put mud in it but I drunk it anyway. I was winning all kinds of money and the bets were still coming in, there was this boy named Anthony and he bet me 10 dollars that I would not slap this big boy named Gary in this face. I walked right up to Gary and slapped him in the face and I was a little fellow so I took off and everyone said I ran away from faster than a horse and then Anthony said he is crazy too and Anthony said let's call him crazy horse and that name stayed with me the rest of my life.

Gary is Mad

I got to school the next and everyone said Gary was looking for me so I tried to stay out of the way of him but I didn't know where he was so I had to be careful. I made it through the first couples of classes with no problem but when recess came Gary caught me from behind and choked me out and then he punched me in the and then threw me into the garbage can and walked off. Everyone in the school laughed at me I didn't care I had me 10 dollars so I didn't really care. Everyone at school thought I was hurt bad, but I climbed out of the garbage without even being hurt. Everyone was taking about how tough I was and from that day on I was the class clown but as long as they were laughing at what I was doing and not at me I was just fine.

Trouble at Home

When I got home, Juanita was mad because she got a call from the school about me fighting and taking other kids' money. Juanita was so mad she went through my room but this time she did not find anything because I had it hid good, but still she got me on the fighting, so I was in trouble either way. This time it was my fault but I told Juanita that the he was picking on me for nothing, but for some reason she did not believe me because she said I would not get no more allowance until I did better but what she didn't know I had about 25 dollars hidden in the back of my closet.

The one thing she did not want was hit me and I'm glad because my body was sore from the beating Gary gave me and my body told the story but any little guy would not dare to mess with me, and all I heard when I walked down the hall or go outside this boy was crazy or there goes crazy horse and every time that I heard that it made me worse, because I know everyone was waiting on a show and every day I tried to give them one.

Time to Take A Swim

It was finally the end of the school year and was playing around and failed one class math by 2 points, so I had to go to summer school because I wanted to play football. When I went to summer school, I made all good grades something I could have did in the first place, because the work I did I already knew. I got Donnie and Daniel and Melissa that was Donnie's girlfriend at the time but anyway we went swimming at ever back road creeks that Donnie could think of and some of them had bridges and he would dare me to jump off and I would every time. I found a rope tied to a tree and grabbed it and it made me swing to the middle of the creek and went almost to the bottom and I did not come up right then I wanted them to look for me. Donnie the rest of the people there do not know what to do but I came up on the other side behind a tree and was killing myself laughing hard but when someone said they were going to call the police I came from behind that tree and everyone was mad but happy I was ok.

Time to Ride

Donnie came and picked me up and wanted to ride so I said lets ride and it was the same ones riding as before and we went everywhere because both of us had money because I kept a scam going one way or another because these people around here was not ready for me because the hand is quicker than the eye unless you try to fool me. We went to this store in Amory to get some gas and I told Donnie I had it and I went in the store and it was full and it was going be awhile before I could pay for my gas so I waited for a minute and just walked out and went back to the car and told Donnie I paid for the gas and we drove and nobody ever knew nothing.

I remember gas was about 90 cents a gallon so we road all night and because I paid for the gas Donnie had to buy the food and drink the whole trip no matter where we went and the next tank of gas was on someone else because I spent all my money on the first tank of gas so they thought. I was so smart that I really didn't need money because I would walk in the store and take what I wanted just like my uncle Robert showed me and now I did it just because I could or that is what I needed at the time. I didn't what I had to steal or who I had con I was going to get what I wanted one way or another.

Too Much Fun

When I was hanging out Juanita and David told me to be home before dark, so I played smart and hung out with David almost all-day playing basketball and football with David and Juanita's brothers George and Terry. I had already talked to Donnie early and we had 3 girls that wanted to meet us at Tupelo MS and for you that don't know that was about 20 miles from where we were no big deal expect for the time but I that took care of. I had a lot of fun already but my day has just begun, I told David that I was tired and ready to bed this was about 7:30pm so I went in my room and went right to sleep with my music on. I woke up about 9:00pm and got some pillows and got some clothes and I made it look like I was in bed but I was gone out the window and then I had to wait on George to come outside we almost got left because Donnie thought we was not going. We got to Tupelo and we road around for a while looking for them girls and finally, we met them, and they ask do we like to play basketball because that was where everyone was hanging out.

We were not doing nothing else so went and hung with the girls and got on the court and 3 on 3 to show out for the girls and then we hung out some more and then we started home and looked up and Juanita and her Mom was in the car right beside us and I knew that I was in trouble but it was about 12:30 at this point and I had the best time of my life just being a kid, so whatever I had coming to me was ready to take it.

Trying to get Home

Donnie was giving that car everything he could trying to get us home, because it was already about 12 or 1 in the morning and I climbed in my window I knew I was good, but as soon as I got in my window the lights to my room came on and I was so scared I started to jump back out the window but I saw it was David and Juanita and then I really wanted to jump out side and keep going. Juanita said they saw George and Donnie in the car but didn`t see me so they waited to catch me red handed because Linda saw George seek out but they didn`t see me but they knew George was not going to nothing wrong without me. It was our code that way we could watch each other's back so that is how I got caught. This time they were serious, David told me to bend over and he gave me about 10 licks on the butt with a belt and I got grounded for 2 weeks but that was still better than that bullwhip so I would good with anything else.

I still remember the hurt on David`s face as he had to whip me, I started to tell him that it was alright but I was trying to get out of trouble so I went to bed like I was told the first time, but really, I did go to bed the first time but I got right back up. I had a good talk with George about how to seek out of the house without getting caught and when he gets caught keep your mouth shut and from that day on, we were good.

Family Time

David and Juanita spend a lot of time with me and I knew that loved me because they have not sent me away let or tried to kill me but I am not going to lie I was out of hand with a lot of things I was doing but I was doing them to fit in and to make people laugh. The thing I liked the most was Juanita`s family was right next door and I could come over any time I wanted either through the front door or the back door or through the back window that lead to the boy's room and before me meeting these kids they were so nice and listen to their parents and everything and about 2 months with them kids and they are acting just like me, but they got beat down and I went home. I forgot to tell them that part sometimes when you bow up you will get knock out but that is how you live and learn the hard way. I really loved living there it was the most fun a kid could ever have because David would get out there and play football or basketball with us and most of the time he would win and I can say David was really a good guy always tries to help someone in need, because he helped me more than 1000 times and he is there to help me with one more time if I really needed it.

David did not play any foolish and what he said he meant and that went a long way with me and I just want to stop and say thank you and to Juanita and my Mom and everyone that help me in my life and most of all I want to thank God because without HIM I am nothing in the first place. I know even today God has a plan for my life and I just pray I can live up to it.

Loved to Scam

I loved to run a scam because it was so easy for me do, and I did it to see if I could get away with it. My uncle Robert showed me how to get what I wanted without paying for it, he was the slickest thing that I have ever saw and he taught me well. I could go into a store and take what I wanted and never get caught it was so fun to me. I wanted some baseball cards and I did not want to pay for them because I knew I could get them for free, so I went in the store and put 10 packs of cards in my pants and walked out and no one knew nothing.

I had to sell the baseball cards to have more money to shoot dice and to run other scams I thought of, and as long as the other kids thought they had a chance to get my money that was all I needed. I would always say the hand is quicker than the eye, and in the brink of an eye that is how long it would take me to scam you.

The Amory Bridge

I recall everyone was mad because I kept winning everyone's money on every bet someone would make me, so the next big bet was I would not jump off the Amory bridge so I told them to make their bet, and the bet was 50 dollars and a case of beer. The people that went was Donnie and Melissa that was Donnie's girlfriend and Donnie's younger brother Daniel and to make everything fair we had a camera where Daniel could take the picture if I jumped off the bridge. We were all drinking beer and I was going to put on a show, so I got on top of the bridge and looked down and saw how high it was and right then and I changed my mind, but I still wanted to put on a show. I climbed over the rail and stepped on concrete block on the side wall high in the air and kept acting like I was going to jump, and everyone stopped, and said I was going to jump and kill myself.

The whole thing was funny to me, so I would get off the bridge and go get me another beer and let the cars pass. It was the funniest thing that I had ever done, and this went on for about 30 minutes, and the more I did it the more fun it was. I got back on top of that bridge and looked down and there were 2 nice looking girls in a boat and they ask me was I going to jump and I said I was thinking about it and they said if you do they would give me some. I was showing out for the girls and slipped off the bridge and I tried to grab the top but it was too late back I started to fall, and all I could say was God I just killed myself, and I had a life jacket on but I still went about 30 feet under and came back up.

The boat with the girls in it took off and it felt like ribs were broke, so I called for Donnie to come and help me but all he did was laugh, so I had to dog paddle back to shore. My body was as red as the sun, so by the time I got my shirt on the police showed up and ask who was jumping off the bridge and I said there is no one crazy enough to jump off that bridge he went that way, and I pointed toward Amory. The police told to get the hell out of there, so we got our stuff and got out there, and the good thing was that Daniel got to take the picture so at least I had that.

I Need My Money

When I got to Okolona, I had to go find Brad and his brother, because they are the ones that bet me, but when I found them, they did not want to pay. Brad said that is no way I jumped off that bridge and lived to tell about it, so he really didn't want to pay me but after I showed him that picture and told him that if he didn't pay me that we was going to fight, so Brad and his brother got my money together and they paid me. I was really glad that he gave me my money because my body was already hurt, and I don't know how much more pain I could take. I got my money and my beer so that helped me a little bit, but I got say I would not jump off that bridge again for all the money in the world.

Words Travel Fast

I remember I jumped off the bridge on a Saturday, and by Monday the whole school had heard of me jumping off that bridge and everyone was talking about it. I was famous overnight, and it felt great, but still people were laughing at me but at this point I did not care. I done something that no one else ever did and till this day no one still has not done it, so that is my bridge, because even today when I pass that bridge I think about that day and no one can ever take that day from me. There was all kinds of people coming up and asking me about me jumping off the bridge and some of these people did not even go to school and to make things even better Donnie had the picture to show I was telling the truth, so my life at that time was so great and the legend of crazy horse really just begin.

The Birthday Juanice

    Juanita and David were having a baby and I just knew that my sister and I would love her very much. I really didn't know who to feel because with new baby in the house I knew there would be no time for me, but I was wrong because they loved me just the same. I can truly say that no matter what went in my life or how bad I messed up, I could always count on Juanita and David, they are my heart and soul because with the chips was down them two was my first call. Juanice was a blessing for me because she took up more of their time so I could get away with more, but if I crossed that line I sure to be put back in line quick. Juanice was so loved and it was great to have a 3rd little sister, so all could say was welcome to the family.

Chapter 12

A Lot of Free Time

It was summer time and there was no school so I had a lot of free time, and most of the time I was with Donnie because he was my best friend and he had a car so I could move around, and we use to get in a lot of crazy things together and boy was it fun. We used to go to water park but most the time we went to the mall to check out the girls or just to hang out because there was nothing else to do. I knew how to hustle so I always had money for what I needed and if not, I would go in the store and take what I wanted. I remember one time I went to Tupelo and I wanted to get some new baseball cards from Fred's so I went in the store saw the cards and then put them down my pants and started to walk out of the store, but all at once some man told me to stop so I took off running with some man right behind me, and then when I looked up there was the police and that was all she wrote because I had nowhere to run because I was boxed in, so I just got on the ground and the police put the handcuffs on me and took me to jail, but I was under age so all they could do was call my parents to come get me but I would felt safer in jail.

Went to Memphis

I got in so much trouble after going to jail. When Juanita got there she said they should have kept me in jail but I was too young, so I got to go home with David and Juanita and when I home I was in so much trouble and I was grounded so that meant not going anywhere until about a month. I told David I was walking to the store, which I did and Donnie stayed right across from the store and he yelled and said come here so I went over to see what he wanted and he said he was going to Memphis. I said lets go so we headed for Memphis it was fun trip and when we got in Memphis we saw a sign that read baseball cards show and meet the great Micky Mantle about 10 miles up the road, you know I had to go because I enjoyed looking at cards and trying to sell mine, because I always had my book of cards with me all the time. I walked around to find someone that did not know that much about cards and try to sell them some of my cards for higher price than I paid for it. I wanted to get Micky Mantle to sign a ball or something, but the line was too long, and it cost 50 dollars, so I had to wait. Donnie went around and tried to sell enough cards to buy a ball signed by Micky Mantle, I came up and set my album of cards right of top of a box of diamond kings which was worth a lot of money if you find the right card in the pack. I looked around for a minute and then I said I guess I would walk around, and then I picked up the box of cards with my cards and then walked away. I hurried up and took the cards to the car and me and Donnie opened up the cards in the car, and we found a Barry Bonds diamond king the was worth over 400 dollars, we went back to that same dude and sold him that card for 300 dollars and he was happy to pay it. We got the ball signed and went to see Travis Tritt and Marty Stewart it was the best time ever. For me I loved knowing that trip was on the man at the card shop, because like I said my hands was quicker than the eye. This is something now I'm not proud of but then it was really fun

In Trouble Again

I got in a lot of trouble after I went to Memphis without telling anyone and I was already grounded, so that just made it worse. I got made go see the psychiatrist but that still did not mean I had to talk to him about my life or what was going on in it, because I had my own way to deal with that. David took me to his office and waited outside in the waiting room while I and the psychiatrist talked, and all he was saying was if I cut the grass I would feel part of the family, I was already cutting the grass that did not have nothing to with it.

The more I talked to that guy the crazier I thought he was the crazy one, so he got mad because I would not talk to him and told me to wait outside while he talked to David. David went in and talked to the good Doctor and about 5 minutes David came out and said this man is crazy let's go and I was to glad to get out of there. I remember I and David laughed about that crazy man all the way home, and that man's crazy talk somehow brought me and David closer.

No More School

Everyone was ready for school but I just found out the school didn't want me at school anymore, and the only way I found out was that Juanita did not buy me school clothes for the next school year and I ask her what was going on and she said the school didn't want me anymore at school, I was too bad and that was that. I had a lot of free time to do what I wanted, and most of the time me and George would just walk the streets just to have something to do. We would walk around town all night and that sometimes you get us in trouble because we would get blamed for stuff, we had nothing to with. Every time something would get stolen or a house get broke into, they blamed us, and we never had anything to with none of that. The police would see us walking around and just think we was up to no good, but we didn't care we just kept walking because no one back then told me what to do because I was ten foot tall and bulletproof and nothing could hurt me.

The Pool Hall

The pool hall was the only thing to do in Okolona, so me and George would hang out during the day and we thought we was so cool but kids today how cool is it to be 40 and don't know nothing but how to shoot pool and pick up garbage, it is a tough life without your education. Thanks to the good Lord I made it but why would anybody want to start in the whole in life like I did. I was the one of the best poll shooters there was in Okolona because all I had to do was to shoot pool all day and night and this was something, I was good at and loved to do. I would bet whatever I had to just pay to play the next game no matter what it cost me, but I always had a rule if someone was that much better than me I would just quit and live to fight another day. Me and George kept a lot of people in the pool hall just to see if they could beat us but most of the time if would always end in the same way with me taking your money.

Time to Go

I was just hanging out all day with nothing to do and Juanita and David was mad, so they said I had to find so where else to live when I turned 18 and that was about a couple weeks away but I thought they was playing, but the joke was on me because after my birthday the next day my stuff was on the porch and Juanita said I had to go. I did not go too far because David had a traitor right beside the one we was staying in and Juanita's mother stayed right beside us too so I was good but George and his sister and a friend of the family wanted to go to Florida, so we all got our money together and we moved to Florida. We hit the highway and just like that I was gone.

Life in Florida

When we all got to Florida and we had a ball, we did not have anybody to tell us what to do, and I knew how to go to the store or where ever to get something to eat or to pay the rent. There was always something going on and people coming over giving us things and one dude left his door open and told us to help ourselves, so when we got hungry, we would just help ourselves to his food. We could walk to the store or the beach in no time and check out the women or go to the movies and check out some women, the women was everywhere your eyes could see and almost wearing nothing it was like being at spring break this was the life. We could sleep as long as we wanted and stay up as late as we wanted and party all night and no one could say anything to us like I said this is the life. I remember stealing this man's lawn motor out of his yard and sanding it down and painted it and then cut his grass with the same lawn motor the next day. I remember getting back to our house and just killing ourselves laughing about what we just did, but that was how everyone else was doing so I just got in line and got mine.

Time to Work

It was time to pay rent and we had to walk

down to this work temp service to see if they had work for me or George, and the first couple of times we went they had nothing for us to do, but on the 3rd day they found work for George but not for me, so I went to work cutting grass and stealing what was on the outside and taking it to the pawn shop. I would make more money than George, but the only thing was his was legal and mine was not, but I did not care I did what I wanted too. I went and paid the rent and after that we got some food and beer and after that we were good for the week. This was the best time ever because we could do what we wanted, I met this dude named Brad and we had been hanging out for a few days stealing lawn motors and things left outside and Brad had an idea to break into this old man`s house because he had plenty of money.

When night time came I met Brad in front of that man`s house but once we got there Brad said are you sure because if we get caught that is 20 years in prison, and God said to just go home so I told Brad that I was not going to do it so I just went home, even back then God was watching over me and it is a good thing because I would have been in prison or dead so thank you God.

Time to Leave Florida

The way I seen it I had a nice time in Florida but it was about time to go back home to Okolona but Doris was not ready to go so went to this party

George invited to by these girls and when we came back we called Juanita's Mother to come pick us up, and in no time she was there and we put our things in the car and we was gone. We had a nice time on the way back to Okolona and when we got back everything was just about the same. When I got home I saw just how good I had it in a small town where you know everyone and they know you, and so I said it was time for me to get a job, so George got me a job at this furniture place building chairs but that was not for me. I tried to build them chairs but I could not get the hang of it, so I told them that I was going to use the bathroom and just kept right on going because that job was not for me.

A Great Job

I was looking around for a job and this man at church named Mr. Billy and he was a brick mason and very good at it. I was working outside and got to do work that was not that hard but it was steady, first your got set up the scalpel and then mix the mud, and then you go to take 2 tunnels of brick in each hand, but for some reason I liked it. I made good money, and I was off when it rained this was the perfect job for me. I could walk to his house because he lived on the next street over, I could see his house from mine. It was not long, and I had a car of my own, things are going really well, and my boss would love to go fishing and take most of the day off, so I loved that too. David and Juanita got a divorce and me and David and Juanice moved about a mile from where we were, so we had to get moved in so we a lot going on.

Ready to Ride

I had a car and a job so I could go where ever I wanted to go, so I had this buddy Mike and we have been friends most of our life, so I went and picked him up and then he called some girls so we got the beer and we was ready to ride. Mike told me that I had the best looking one so I called her up and she sounded sexy, so I told her that I would pick her up. I get to her house go up and knock on the door and ask for Lisa and this big girl answers the door she had to weigh 350 pounds and said I'm Lisa, so I still ask her was she ready to go but I was not happy. I could have taken this other girl that was fine, but Mike set me up because he knew what she looked like from the start.

We all decided to go this bar in Pheba Mississippi because you could get something to eat and drink at the same place. Mike was killing himself laughing but I still was nice but I had to tell her what happen and we get to the bar I would pay for her food and drinks but we was not together, and she was fine with because she did not like me anyway. The night ended up great me and Mike both went home with women that night, but I told Mike one day I going to get him because that was one dirty trick.

Crazy Night

I met this girl named Cynthia and we hit it off from the start, I felt an instinct bond with her and this was only the first time that we really met, but I still was taking it slow. Mike and I met 2 girls earlier that night and we hung out with them all night. The bar we were in was closing so we went to the next bar down the road and we are already was feeling good but still wanted to show these women a good time. The first bar we went was okay but Christy that was the girl Mike was with was too loud and acting too crazy for that bar, so we got kicked out after the first drink. We went to next one it was already loud so we was good, and we did some kind of partying, we took shots of whiskey and we drank a lot of beers, and I won about $300 dollars on the pool table, so our night is going good so far. It is about 12:30 and now we need something to eat, so we went to West Point to this little place that open all night.

We all sit down and got ready to order our food and these girls which we knew but not like that, they were from Okolona and they were loud mouths. I don't what their problem was with Christy but when they came to our table Christy kicked over the table and hit one of the girls with a plate, me and Mike was trying to break it up and then the owner came and said get down and when we did there was glass and food all over the place.

Going to Jail

When we all left the restaurants we had one thing on our mine and were getting out of there and fast, I remember we ran and got in the car and I took off, so as soon as we got around the counter I saw the police in my mirror. I started to keep on going but I knew that would be more trouble so I just pulled over, when the police came up the car I was so scared because I did not know what was going to happen, but when the officer came to the a was cool, and told us to follow him back to the police station so that what we did. When we got to the police station they ask everyone what happen and then the officer told us the owner said the same thing that the other people started it, so they told us to get to where ever we was from, so we hurried up and got out of there. I thanked God that day because I knew we was all going to jail, so we went to their house in the middle of nowhere that where we stayed because we didn't want to push our luck anymore that night.

Time Well Spent

I was spending a lot of with Cynthia and it was time well spent, I use to go to West point every night after she would get off and pick her up or sometimes I would just meet her at her house. We were really good for each other, but her family didn't like me because they thought I was black, but I didn't care because I was falling in love. I went and got me a job at the city of Okolona working for water department things was looking up, and now I could buy her something real nice for her birthday. I got her some flowers and a card and took her out to eat, it was one great day because the rest of the day we cannot talk about that but like I said it was time well spent.

Time to Fight

We have been going together for about 2 months and I found out that her old boyfriend was trying to get back with her and I went off, so got his number out of her phone and called him and told him to meet me at the grave yard in West point. I called my boy Sam; he was a Mexican and he loved to fight so I got him to keep things even. We loaded up, it was Cynthia and Tasha, and Tasha was Sam`s women and she was just as bad as him and then there was me and I was mad. I was drinking the whole way there to get my head right and was playing eye on the tiger to get me pumped up.

When we got to the graveyard I got out of the car and told him who I was and punched him in the face and he hit the ground and then I got on top on him and then choked him out. I told him to get up and get the hell out of there and don`t come back, and Sam was standing there watching the other boy that came and he took one look at Sam and didn`t want to try nothing. I always hate to have to fight but if you push me, you would always get what you was looking for, but to tell you the truth I would much whether me making love than fighting anyway.

A Night on the Town

Sam and I and the girls all wanted to go out because we had not been out in a while after what happen the last time we went out, but this time we chose a quiet place where there would be the least likely to get in trouble. We went to the movies but there was nothing we wanted to see, so we decided to walk around the mall but when we started to walk in the mall they told us we had to leave because they had Sam`s picture up and if he comes back he would go to jail for trespassing, so we hurried up and got out of there. It seems like most of the people I hung out with was just like me, because everywhere I went trouble was not too far behind or already waiting on me. We went to bowling alley and we didn`t have any more problems and the night turned out good, because we ate pizza and drank beer until about 12 am and then went home, it was the best night ever.

A Great Life

I guess the old saying is true, you really don`t know how happy you can be until you fall in love. I knew there was something special about this girl and I think she feels the same way, but sometimes in life you never know. I was about 20 years old and got a girl and a car, to me life was so great, sometimes I wonder where that person went to because now when I look back I don't really know where that crazy boy went. I use go to the bar and drink almost every night but know that I have got older if I do drink most of the time if I do it is at the house, it is so funny how life can change. I loved this girl so much, but I don't know if she loves me back, not enough to get married but who knows anything could happen. I took her to the finest restaurant in town and already got her a $500 ring and so half way through dinner I ask her to marry me but I didn't get down on one knee, but she still she said yes. I just got my own house and I going to get married so like I said my life is great.

My First Real Love

    I felt like I was on cloud nine, because everything was going so great, and this was my first true love and everybody else was just playing or just wasting your time. This was true love and there was nothing better than that and knowing someone else loves you, it makes you feel like you had a million dollars and that is the best feeling in the world. When she was off work we was together and when I was off we was together, so that meant we spent a lot of time together so much that we stayed at each other's house a lot at night, so that meant I had to get up early but she was worth it. One day I got off work and tried to call my girl and she would not answer so I went over there and when I got there I saw another car in her car and I came unglued, I beat on the door but no one would come out, but I stayed there about 2 hours waited on this dude to come out. I got a call said you wanted to meet so I loaded up and went to hear, when I got there we had a real talk and she told me that she was going to get married to her old boyfriend that was in the military, and she didn't mean to hurt me, and said I was sad but it was better for me to know how she feels before we get married, so just like that our life together was over.

No More Love

I just got my heart broke and was not in the mood to fall in love again, so I started telling women what they wanted to hear to get I wanted just like they did me. The day we broke up was the day something change inside me because my eyes was open to how the world really was, the only real person that I could count on was myself and sometimes I would let myself down. I met up with Mike and he wanted to go to New Orleans and really didn't have anything going on and it was close to Christmas so I said lets go and just like that we jumped in the car and was gone. We took turns driving and only stopped when we needed gas or something to eat. I was drinking beer the whole way, but I had it in a cup, so no one knew what I was drinking. We made it to New Orleans and got to the store it was about 11pm and I was out of beer but I knew I was going to have to wait till the next day but Mike said you can buy whiskey and beer all-night so I got something to drink and I was ready to go.

Fun All Day

I finally made it to where Mike's Mothers house was and I saw a lot of things in that town, I saw a man that was 12 feet tall and people standing like a statue, it was the craziest thing I have ever seen. I was walking around in amazement not knowing what bar or club I wanted to go in first, I think I must have gone to 20 clubs before I just had enough and just went home. I woke up the next the day and started over again, this time I had got a friend of Mike's to go with me and how could I say no because she looked pretty good. I went from side of New Orleans to the other it was great, we talked and we went to the French Quarter and they even had vibrant live- Music scene and round the- clock nightlife, this place had it all.

We caught a taxi and went to Jackson Square and took a picture by the canon and saw everything there was to see and then we went back to Bourbon street and got a drink at this place called The Beach on Bourbon it had live music and the best DJ`S in the world, it was the best time a person could and the food was like nothing you have ever eaten in Mississippi. It was getting late so I was getting tired so we took a taxi and went home, so I thank her for showing me a good time and gave her a kiss and went home, but that was the best day ever.

Steven "Crazy Horse" Edwards

Chapter 13

One More Day in New Orleans

This was the last day of fun in New Orleans and I had to make it worth my wild, so I went right back to Bourbon Street and did it all over again. We went to all the bars and then me and Mike drove around and seen the rest of the City and then I went to Boomtown Casino and had the time of life. The good thing about New Orleans was that it never shuts down, so you can party as much as you wanted, and no one will bother you. I was walking around and then we saw Mike`s friend and she went with us too, and everyone was trying to show me everything in New Orleans, so we was going into this clothing store and I had a beer in my hand so I was trying to drink it before I went into the store but Mike said you could bring the beer in and when we got inside the store other people was drinking beer too. I saw a sign that read if you spill anything of the clothes you have to buy it and some of them price tags was not cheap, and after that we went to Mike`s moms house and went to sleep, and the next day we woke up and went back to Okolona and we laughed the whole way home.

Saw My Mom

When I came back from New Orleans my mom called my house phone and wanted to meet up and just talk or just spend some time with her. I could not wait to see my mom, because have not seen her in a while and I had a lot of questions for her. I was about 13 the last time saw my mother and now I'm 22 so you could say it has been a long time. First we went to Wendy's and got something to eat and we had a good time just talking and enjoying each other company, and my mom brought her boyfriend to meet me , he was not too bad, he said he loved my Mother so that good enough for me. We went to the movies just to spend more time with her, this was a day I would remember for the rest of my life, and because I got to spend it with my mom after all the time we spent apart. I ask my mom why she left us like she did and she told me that she did not have a choice, because the DHS was going to put us in a foster home so she did not have a choice in the matter. I wish she would have given us to our Granddad, but things did not turn out that way, and that was a hard lesson learned that life don't always turn out your way.

Never Apart Again

I spent to whole day with my mom and her boyfriend and we had a good time but not all the things was said was happy, but we just said what we was feeling because that is how close we are. I think that day we got closer than we had ever did in the past because we laid it all on the line and said what needed to be said and I did it without hurting her feeling so I think I did good. My Mom was getting ready to go and before she did I got her phone number and where she lived so I could go find her, so I gave her a kiss and told her I loved her and then she was gone, but from that day own we kept in touch, but I hope my mother knows that I never stop loving her.

Time for Love

I was in Houston MS and I was at the pool hall on Main Street, and I saw this woman and she was so beautiful, she had long black hair, this one was just my type and I was going to talk to her. I walked over and told her my name and she told me her name was Tracy and her ride was not there to take her home, so I took her to her house and met her dad. I knew that she was something special and I just knew that she was the one. We hung out for the next 2 weeks and we was really getting serious and I wanted her to move in with me, so we talked about it and it seem like a good idea so she moved in with me. This was one of the best days of my life because for once I did something right, and for once I was really happy.

One Cool Dude

It was the weekend and Tracy wanted to go have lunch with her brother and then he was going to hang out with us for the weekend, and when we got there he was cool, it was like we knew each other all my life. Matt was a person that loves to party, and I did not find too many people that could out drink him. We became good friends right from the jump, and this was one person that I could count on many years to come. We would drink 2 bottles of Jose Cuervo with no problems and still ready to drink some more, it was some good time. Matt would bring his girlfriend and sometimes we would double date, we would go to the movies or we would go bowling or sometimes we would just ride around or go hang out with their family, it did not matter what we did we had fun. We would ride the back roads and drink but Tracy would always have to drive because we would get too drunk and didn't need to be behind the wheel but no matter what we had fun and had each other's back.

A First Time for Everything

I have done everything in my life except for getting marriage and having a kid and now I'm going to cross one of them off my list. I got down on one knee and ask her to marry me and she said yes, so I hope this time turns out better than the first time. I knew this time was the real deal because she would go everywhere, I went, and we could not wait until we were back together in each other arms. I was thinking we have been together for about 3 years so I know it was time to get married and Tracy loved me and wanted to get married so bad and I knew in my heart we was ready. I was only 26 but I knew it time to make her my wife, but I made her have to find her ring by leaving clues where to find the ring, and she found it that was the happiest day of her life.

I Messed Up

I was so happy that I was going to get marriage that I was telling everybody about it, and I could not stop smiling because I just found true love. Matt and I went to Houston to hang out at my buddy's house, and when I got to the house there was this crazy girl and to this day, I wish I had never met her. To make a long story short we all went to the bar and then we were feeling good and we were talking and she said she didn`t know anyone and she was leaving in the morning to go to Memphis and would not be back. I know I should not have done anything but the girl was almost naked so we hooked up, and after that she told me that she was Matt cousin and then I said so you must be Tracy`s cousin too and said yes. When she said yes, my heart fell to the floor because I knew I really had messed up and it was going to take some doing to get out of this. When you got a good woman you need to try to hold on to her, because you do not find a good woman walking around every day, so if you get one you better hold her tight.

Two Weeks to Count Down

It was 2 weeks until I get marriage I was so nervous because this other girl would not leave me alone, and she said if I did not keep hooking up with her she was going to tell her cousin, so I had to do what I had to. I finally got tired of that and told her that was enough, and I did not want to see her anymore, so I got in my truck and drove off and that was the end of that. I really was not a good guy, it was like I said I was pretty bad even when I tried to be good, somehow trouble would always find me. It was the night before my wedding and both of my brothers in laws was with me and we just rode around and drinking but Rob was the designated driver and Matt and I was in the back of truck so at first we went to the pool hall and that was where we met that girl again, and she told me that she was going to show up at the wedding, so she said she was coming to the wedding if I didn't go with her, so I dropped off the guys and I went with her. I woke up just in time to get to breakfast before Tracy got there, I was so scared that I could not eat.

My Big Day

This was the best day of my life but also the scariest day of my life, because I just knew that this crazy girl was going to show up, so I was so nervous that I was drinking all day and I still could not get drunk. This was one great day because we rented out the Okolona park it had a swimming pool and everything, but of course we did not use the pool because we were at a wedding but like I said it was nice. We had our whole family, my brother David was there he was my best man, because David has always been there for me no matter how stupid I was or how many crazy things I got myself into David was always there, and that is the reason he was my best man plus he was my dad, so that 2 things in one, a best man and my dad, who could beat it. I saw a lot of people there my sister Juanice was there and Juanita and Carolyn and Rob and Juanita's sister Linda and her husband Cheyenne was there, and he kept my head right all night. I was trying to hurry up the wedding but there no getting that done so I just went alone with the plan and I'm not going to lie I had the time of my life. Tracy's Mother gave us money for a motel because it was getting late because we had just got through cleaning up and it was time to go. I had gone ahead and put roses and chocolate on the bed and then we made love all-night lone, that was one great day.

Just Got Married

Me and Tracy just got married and things was going great, so everything is going good so far until it all went bad and it went bad quick. Matt was in jail and Tracy went to see him and while see was up there see saw her cousin the one that I hooked up with, but after all the trouble she cost me you could call it more than a hook up. She told my wife the whole story and she went off, because they were fighting right in front of the police station, it was a good thing that Tracy knew the police because they just broke them up and sent them home. When Tracy got home she went off on me but I did not lie because she had the letters I wrote her so really there was no need to lie any further so I just came clean and told her the truth. We had a long talk and we said we was not going to let this end our marriage but after that things just did not feel the same, but I was willing to make it work. I think sometimes in life you can go too far and sorry just don't get it after that.

A Good Thing Gone

I had a real love with Tracy but I traded it for some trash without even knowing it at the time, I should have known better but when you mess with the bull you sometimes you get the horn. I think you should stop and think about what you are doing before you just jumping into anything because somethings in life you do you cannot change. I still remember the day we broke up it was so bad because the love of my life was gone, and I did not know how to get her back. I drove her into the arms of another and it was really nothing I could do but I was mad, I got Matt and we went to this pool hall that she was hanging at and I went off, I got out of my truck with my bat and called this dude out, but he would not come out but he sent his boys and I told that boy if he gets any closer I was going to hit him with my bat. Matt was trying to keep the peace and all I wanted to do was to talk to my wife and if she didn't come out I was coming in that pool hall and I was going to be swing at the first one that came at me, but the good thing was that she came out. We talked and she said she was moving out and that really broke my heart.

Begged and Pleaded

I spent 2 weeks begging and pleading for her to take me back and finally she did, but things did not feel the same no matter how hard we tried. We both agreed that this was something we both could not let go so she packed up her things and took her back to the place she was at, and now I'm mad but mad at myself for letting the great woman get away from me, but like they say you cannot have your cake and it eat to. I guess like every time before it was my fault, and I went too far with no way to fix it. I never thought that things would turn this way or I would not have done it in the first place, but I never thought for one minute that I could lose the love of life, but when someone does not trust you anymore that is what happens just about every time. I guess I wanted to be single and married at the same time and them two things does not do well together. I guess I learned a hard lesson that day but when you play you must be willing to pay the price and sometimes that is more than you are wanting to pay but the cost does not have anything to do with you because of the people you hurt.

Time to Move On

It was time for me to start my new life as a single man but I was mad so I was going to her once and for all, so I went and got with her cousin just to show her that I did not need her, but that was so far from the truth. My family was mad and my sisters could not stand that girl but I did not care because I had already lost the one person that always loved me no matter what, so to tell you the truth I did not really care anyway so it was what it was one you too far like I did. I went as far as moving her in with me trying to get my wife's attention but I soon found out when it over it's over. I knew this girl was crazy but I was about to see just how crazy she was, and the load of problems she brought with her, but really I didn't care anyway but I was thinking if she was what cost me my wife, then I guess I should be with her, because I did not want to lose out both ways. I would get so drunk after work but that did not help because every day I had wake up without my wife and without the life that was meant for me. Men don't throw away a gift from God but a piece of trash in the street.

A New Day

It was a new day and I wanted to start this day different than all the one's before because I was worried about something I could not do anything about, but not any more I was going to find me a new love. I had a good friend his name was James

Hill and he would have you laughing all day long and he would do whatever he could to help you if he liked you, it was a good thing he liked me. I had been working at united furniture for about a year and I had it made at work because all I had to do was to pick up the furniture and take it right in front of me it was so easy because I had a good crew. I had got rid of that girl that cost me so much trouble, it was not easy, but it was something that must be done. I was by myself and James Hill said that he was having a party and his stepdaughter was going to be there and she was single, so I said I would be there if I didn`t go see Tracy. There was a part of me that wanted to be with Tracy but the other part of me deep down in my heart knew after what I did, we would never make it.

Which Way Should I Go?

My heart was torn between a love that was not there anymore and letting that love go, but I didn`t know how to let her go but I knew somehow, I had to. I started down highway 32 and I was at a crossroad in my life, but I did not know it yet. I went down that road not knowing which way I was going to go, but as soon as I got to the folk in the road something told me to take a left, so I took a left. When I got to James Hills house they had some kind of party going on, and when I got there it was a lot of people there but I really looking for one person even though I did not know who I was looking for I still was ready to meet someone. James said Tyla that was James step daughter in law and he said she went to the store to get more beer but they didn't know I brought 2 cases of beer and some whiskey, so I plenty for a party of my own. Tyla got there and she was looking good and James took me over to meet her and her sister Dana both of them was so cool I just felt right in with everybody. We all took shots and talked and just had a good time, so far everything is going great.

A Bond is Made

I and Tyla hung out most of the time at the party and we really did not pay much attention to anybody else because we were caught up in what we were talking about. I was telling her about my life and all she could do was laugh, we were feeling each other this night was going great. It was like I had been knowing this woman all my life, because she was so easy to talk to and so much fun to be around. We only had one problem that she was black and I was white or Mexicana, or something I don't really know for sure but anyway a lot of people was not going to like it but they didn't like me anyway so I was not really worried about that, but anyway she was worth giving everything up for, because without love what do you really got. It was getting late and had drunk a lot of beers and I was feeling good, so Tyla ask me spend the night at her house because some of James friends just came through a road block right down the road, so she said I could wait out the road block at her house, and you know I said yes. We made love all night and we bonded like we knew each forever, because after that night you rarely saw us apart.

My Life is About to Change

My life was about to change and I did not know it yet, because she was coming by my house almost every day or I would go pick at her house and we would go out to eat, it was so much fun and for once I was happy again and really enjoying life. We went to meet her kids and they were some nice kids but I don't think they really liked me yet but they really didn't know me good so I knew it was going to take some time, but the good thing was time is all I really had, because I had it all at one time but lost it all, with one night of unfaithfulness, so I was going to make sure that this did not happen again. I took everything slow with the kids and took time to really know all of them, because I wanted to show them that it was not all about their mother that I really wanted to try to be a family, but we was a long way from that right now but anything can happen.

The Brady Bunch

Well lets meet the kids first there was Ricketa Brady she was the oldest and she was about 12 years old and already grown but she was the quiet type, but she would let you know how she felt and that was okay with me. The next girl was Doris Brady and she had no time for playing around, because she would get you told from the jump and most of the she wanted to be left alone but she really had a heart of gold. The next one was kind of my favorite because Damarcus Brady was the last born and he was a boy so I could be ruff with him, at first he would whine because he knew his mother was going to take up for him, but he would always jump into the car when I ready to go somewhere, but that was okay because if I was around they pretty much got what they wanted.

This Could Be Real

We been hanging out for a while so we wanted to do something special so went out to eat and then we went to see a movie and then we went to a nice motel, but what Tyla didn't know was I already went to motel and put roses and candy the shape of hearts on bed, it was really nice. We spent the whole weekend at the motel and again I knew this was something real and I knew I was not just playing, but still I wanted to make sure so the same thing don't happen like before. I stayed in the traitor park and I thought I was happy until I found out that Tyla was thinking about moving on Highway 32 and I thought it would be okay because I was a little scared because we was getting too close, but I knew in my heart that she was the one, but I still wanted to hang out with the boys. Tyla moved on 32 me and Matt went out to party, so at first we wanted to get something to eat before we went to party, but the more time I spent in the restaurant the more I wanted to be where she was. We got our food to go and we hurried up and got to 32 because I was not going to be happy until I got there.

Home Sweet Home

When I got to her I made sure I told her I felt and that I was tired of playing around so we hung out there and drunk some beers and all that night something inside of me was telling me I was home. I did not know what was wrong with me because all I wanted to do was to spend time with her. I made up my mind that was the place I needed to be, so I stayed. It was not all roses, but we made it work because we loved each other and wanted to be together no matter what. It was a great life and her family already loved me, so I was good. It was time for me to step my game up so I made sure that I paid my part of the bills and I tried to stay around and make her happy, so I made sure I took her out and made sure she had a good time. One day her cousin Lilly was having a party and I we was invited and the good thing about that was you could just walk to her house, it seem like after all this time I was happy again, but you have never went to a party till you went to a party on 32.

Me and JC Hanging Out

I was hanging out with JC and we was having a lot of fun, but I always put her children first, because before we did anything we made sure the kids had everything they needed but after that they had get out of our way because it was grown up time. We would turn the music up and party all night and we used to do this about 3 times in one week, so we were spending a lot of time together, so it did not take us long to bond. JC was someone that could talk you out of your last dime and you really needed it, but whatever you wanted JC would find a way to get it. JC was always the loudest thing in the room but he would always make everyone laugh no matter what he did, but he was not what he said that got me it was what he would do, because he would always say he was not going to help someone and then turn right around and help him. He always tried to help me, because if was not for him I would never meet Tyla anyway, so we had a good time every time we got together. I remember I started to get my life together because this love was a love I wanted to keep because her love was all that was on me at that time.

I Found God

When I was on highway 32, I was in the country, so I did not have the distraction of being in town so had more alone time. I went to church in Van Vleet, Mississippi and this was like no other church before, maybe I just needed to slow down so the Lord could show me He was there the whole time and what He had for my life. I sat down and it was like I knew these people all my life and everyone made me feel right at home. There was a lot of singing and that was so great because most of the songs I heard my Grandmother sung to me when I was a baby, so I knew most of the songs pretty good. They got through singing and now it was time for the preacher to get up there and preach and he was on fire and he had the whole church feeling the Holy Spirit because he was telling us about God's love and how He sent His son Jesus to die for our sins and that He had to power to forgive us of our sins, and I knew all about Jesus but I was told as bad as I had been Jesus would not forgive me anyway. The preacher called for altar call and something inside me told me to go so I went, and boy I'm so glad I did because my life as I knew it was about to change.

Mercy Found Me

When I got to the preacher, I was so nervous my hands were sweating, and my heart was beating so fast, but I had to find out once and for all would God forgive me. I went to preacher and I was in tears because I wanted God to save me too, he asked me did I know God and was I saved and I said no because everyone told me God would not forgive me because of the bad things I did and the preacher ask me who told me that and I said that what I was told all my life. The preacher stopped me right then and told me that was not true and if I didn't believe him then I could try God for myself, so I got down on my knees right then and there and gave my heart to God. It was like the whole wait of the world was lifted off my shoulders and right then a red light went off in my head, if God could save me for what I have done He could forgive and save anybody. That was the first time in a while that I felt like this, but the question was what was I going to do about it?

Time for A Change

It was time for a change and just in time because I just moved into a new house and I wanted to make this love work and now I'm learning about God's love at the same this was a lot to take in at one time but I was going to make it work even though I had failed so many times before, but for some reason this time felt different. I was on 32 and like most of you that read this or know the real me, the one they call crazy horse that I smoked weed and drank beers and I thought that was all to my life, but one day something crazy happen, something inside of me told me to pick a note book so I did and I wrote the most beautiful love poem to Tyla and it was so good it shocked me. I never knew this was the start of something great.

A Death of a Friend

There is a lot of things that was to personal to right down, so that is why certain things in my life that may have happen is not wrote down, so if someone close to me did not get your story in my book I'm sorry but I only have so many pages. I was writing more and more and I myself was amazed with the things I was writing but still I didn't know if anybody would like it. I started writing poems and other things for people, but I was just playing around, but this was something I really was having fun doing. I had this friend from highway 32 his name was Eric and he we was pretty good friends and one day he had a heart attack, I remember it like yesterday Eric was late that morning and he was always on time, but we really didn't think that much about it, so I went on to work. It was about 30 minutes after I got to work Tyla called and said Eric was dead and we just hung out the night before, it was a real big shock to me and the rest of the family and everyone that knew him was so sad.

Helps on The Way

I saw Eric's grandmother and she was heartbroken over the loss of her grandson and I told her how sorry I was because we was starting to get close because Eric was around on our road when he got off work, and we use to sit in the yard and drink or sometimes we would walk down the road to shoot pool at our friend's spot and you could even get a beer while you shoot pool. I remember Eric would always try to help people when he could he was just a good guy to hang out with, so I wanted to help if I could because like I said he was part of our family. I knew I could write something to help that family but I really did not how to do it, so I started the only way I knew how, I got down on my knees and ask the Lord to help me and He did not let me down. I started writing and at the end of the poem I was crying so I knew it was good to me, but I still did not know how everyone else thought yet, so I showed Tyla and her mother and both of them loved it. It was time for the funeral and I was a packed house and everyone there was sad, so the preacher ask if anyone had anything to say , so I stood up and read my poem and the whole church starting crying.

Don't Cry for Me

Don`t cry for me, because all my pain is gone, and my soul can finally go back home. Don`t cry for me, I will be alright, you just try to get your soul right. Don`t cry for me, because I`m going home, to sit with God on His throne. Don`t cry for me, and please don`t look sad; just remember all the good memories we had. Don`t cry for me, or sing any sad old song, because now my soul can finally go home. Mom, don`t cry for me, because I will see you again, but for now, me and the Lord, are going to take it on in.

A Light Went Off

When I got through reading that the whole church starting crying, and after the funeral everyone came up and told me how good that poem was and how touched they was. It was like a red light went off, if I could write something like that and I was just playing, I wonder what I could do if I really try, so right then and there I decided to help people and to put my heart and soul into it. I still remember Eric's grandmother hugging me and thanking me for writing that poem, but I told them that it was not me but the Lord. I knew I could not write nothing like this until God came in my life, so there is no need of taking credit for something I did not do. Then they will ask me did I write this or not and I would tell them God wrote it, but He used my hands and that is okay with me. I thank God for opening up my eyes and showing me that I can do all things with God on my side, and thank Him for forgiving me for all the bad things I did even when I did not deserve it, so this was one way I could give back for all God did for me.

So Much to Do

I was so fired up for the Lord and my soul was on fire because I wanted to tell everyone about the Lord and what he did in my life. My family loved what I writing because most of the poems were wrote about them, but there were other people that I knew nothing about and hit the problem they was dealing with on the first time writing anything down, the poems was so good it amazes me. The only problem I had was the more people I helped, the more people I saw that needed my help and needed to be told about the Lord. I would write down out of the bible and make a lot of copies at United Furniture, by the way thank you for the paper, but anyway I used pass them at Walmart and put them on people's windows, some people did not like it but that was okay because I was not doing it from them I was doing it for the Lord. I remember I was at Walmart passing out papers and a security guard came and told me I could not put them on the windshields and he told me to take them off and I told he wanted them off he would be the one that had to do it, because I put them on every car at Walmart and it was packed because it was Saturday, so I got in my car and went to another Walmart.

A Day at The Mall

I just got from Walmart and Doris and Riccka was waiting on Doris's daddy to take them to the mall and buy them some school clothes but they had been waiting for a while and Doris was crying so I told them to come on because I was going to take them to mall. It was Doris and Riccka and one of their friends and Tyla's son Mark and we was all heading to the mall. We were all at the mall and I had about $1500 dollars and was ready to spend some money on these kids. I told the girls to go the girls store and pick out what they wanted and then come get me and I will come and pay for it. I took Mark to one of the men's store so we could get some clothes and shoes, it was not long me and Mark was already done with our shopping and we were waiting on the girls. I knew something was not right because Riccka came out of the store with her head down and I said what was wrong and she said we spent a little too much money, so I went to see how much it was, and when I saw how it was I almost lost my mine because it was about $250 dollars but I paid it with no problem and that is when the kids knew that could count on me.

The Power of God

I just saw God at work and how much power He really had over my life, but I really did not know what to do with it let. I just starting writing so all I could do was wait on God and see who He wanted me to help and how many more blessing He has in my life. I come to find out that God was with me the whole time, I just didn't know it but God was starting to make it very clear what he wanted me to do. I remember more and more people was coming up to me and asking me to help them and it was fun so I kept doing it, but I saw that something else that was going on people was also getting help by the things I was writing. I saw God at work in my life for the first time but I knew He was there the whole time, but like most of you I really did not think God had time for me, but really it is us that don't have time for Him, and that is a problem that we all need to fix, but first you must learn how. For the first with God showed me how to love again and open up and really help people and for that all praise goes to God.

Restarts Time

I had the chance to restart time because now I could show these kids some love that growing up it seems I missed but got a lot of love when I was real young and with my Mother and Grandparents, but the rest of the time I felt like I was really just in the way and if this hurts someone feelings then I sorry but that was I felt. I do not understand how someone could be mad at me for what I did 30 years ago, when 30 years ago I was just a kid and really did not know what was going in life, but still I would like to say I'm sorry. That is one reason I set out on this mission to tell people about God and what He did in my life. I finally saw the power that God could have on my life if I just trust Him, and now I could show these kids the love that I didn't want or got. It is so crazy that I got the chance to restart time and show these kids that I loved them and was going to be there for them and not just their mother.

Chapter 14

Heading to Washington D.C.

I got a letter in the mail from poetry.com because I was writing poems and was putting them on their site and one of my poems won a contest. I had a chance to win $20,000 and a free book contract, but the only problem was I had to get to Washington DC and I had some money but it was not enough money but I knew if God took me this far He would send me the rest of the way. I prayed to God and ask Him what He wanted to do and He told me to cook plates and sell them and go around and take up money and He will send someone to help me and all I had to was ask and He would do the rest. I had a lot of people from united furniture and a lot other was glad to help me on trip. There was one person that I really want to thank and person is Lilly Shelton because she was always there for me, telling to just keep on and she fixed the plates and brought them to work, she was more than a friend, she was more like my sister we was just that close. We was able to raise the money for the bus and the hotel but we could only raise enough money for a one way ticket, but still the Lord told me to go and He would take care us anything so I went.

A New Look on Life

I rode the greyhound from Tupelo MS all the

way to Washington DC and it took 2 days for me to get there but that was okay because I got to see a lot of this country, I know we went through about 5 states, it really was a great time for me because I got get out of MS, so I was good. I got to DC and it was like I knew the people all my life, because everyone I needed God put them in my place so they could help me. First it started with the hotel manager, I saw how much it was to stay a week in that hotel, so I prayed for God to make away and when I got the counter and told the manager what I was doing and how much money I had and he took it and all I could say was thank God and keep on my way knowing God had everything under control. There were a lot of people at poetry contest, one of the people there was Mickey Rooney and he told me that my work sounds good but I need it in to get into book form and he would buy one, so that gave me a lot of confidence because that was only the first day, so that gave me a new look on life because now my book was actually a real thing because Mickey Rooney said it was good.

I Saw the Light

The second day at DC was better than the first because I finally saw for the first time how rich I really was but sometimes you have to see what someone else does not have to appreciate the things you have. I was eating dinner at McDonald`s and I saw this lady get through with her food and threw the rest in trash and this bum grabbed the food out of garbage can and ate it. I walked over to him and told him that God loved him and then I brought him a burger and then I sat down and wrote a poem and it was called what kind of plan and I will write it down on the next page. To make a long story short I was praying for this man and asking God to show God this man's life plan, it was the lowest feeling I had in my life because I was always complaining about what I did not have and for what I could not see that other people had nothing and no place to stay and nothing to eat but when you are caught up in your world, it is real hard to worry about someone when you are caught up in your own problem.

God What King of Plan

God kind of plan is for this man to eat food out of garbage, it sounds like a joke, but man is really broke. God how is this plan right, this man does not have a place to sleep at night, he does not want to rob, but has given up on life and getting a job, God please take this man a show him his life plan. I tell you that little moment with that man really changed my whole life and how I went about doing thing in my life, and especially when came to complaining about what I did not have or the house I was living in, because these people lived on the streets and was not complaining, but I stayed in a 3 bedroom house and had two cars and money to buy food when I wanted it and still I was complaining, so I had to stop and ask myself what was I complaining about. The point I wanted to make was to be thankful for what you have and don't worry about the things you do not have because a lot of things in this world you do not need anyway.

I Saw God's Plan

I was ready to do whatever for God after I met that homeless man that was eating out of the garbage can, so I trust God if He wanted me to do something for him then He must help me. I went all over DC telling people about the Lord but the more people the more that needed my help it was a great time to get to work for the Lord. I prayed to God to help me and he did, not only did I win a medal but I won a trophy that said that I was one of the best writers in this contest it really didn't pay that much because I didn't win the big money but still it was good to win something.

I made a lot of friends but I guess the craziest one was this woman at the bus station and she said she was scared for life, so she stayed around me until her bus came because she said I made her feel safe, I know God sent that lady to me. I had been in DC for about a week and I walked over most of that town and looked and seen a lot of the sights, but I was ready to go but I was almost out of money, so I had to wait for my wife at the time to wire me the money for the ticket.

A New Look on Life

I saw how good my life really was after seeing how bad off other people really had it, but that is how it goes in life we set around and complain about what we don`t have and after we think about it we really did not need it anyway. I had to learn to be happy with what I had and not worry about what I did not have, and I believe that is the key to happiness in life. I started telling people more about God and what He did in my life and then I got a letter from the poetry contest saying they wanted to do a best of the best of 2002 so I picked one of my best poems out and sent it in and just like that my poems was in a book, I was so proud and for once things in my life was starting to look up, so I felt like this was my calling own my life because it was so easily to do and it was something I loved doing.

The Power of God

When I was waiting for my ticket to go home the lights went out, but not just our lights it was a blackout in the whole city of DC and there people upset, so God told me to talk to each person at the bus station, I did not know what to do but I did it anyway. I talked to this older lady first because she was crying and I asked her why she was crying and she told me that her daughter was going on another bus and she might not ever she her again, so I ask her which one was her daughter and she said the brown head girl with the blue sweater so I went up and introduced myself to her and told why I was there. I just really ask her one simple question, what you would do if you get on the bus and something happens to your mother what then and right then the girl broke down starting crying and went and traded her bus ticket in for a ticket to wherever her mother was going it really made me feel good. I went around the whole bus station and did that plus there was a lost crazy women that was hanging around me because she didn't want to be by herself and after I got through helping the last person then they called my name to go home and the lights came back on, I could see the power of God at work.

On My Way Home

I got on that bus and I was really ready to get back home, don't get me wrong DC is a great place to visit but that old saying is true, there is no place like home. I was on fire for the Lord and I on the bus telling everyone about it and it was the best feeling that I ever had in my life. I was on the bus with a suit on and preaching God's word and helping people at the same time, it was if God took over my body and was saying all these amazing things, to tell you the truth I was amazed at what I was saying and it was coming out of my mouth. It just goes to show if you let God take control, he will do some amazing things in your life. I finally got close to Okolona and I told the bus driver to let me off right here in Wren and I called Tyla to come pick me up, I was so happy to see my family and my home, and I really needed a bath and a home cooked meal

A New Man

When I got back from DC my soul was on fire and could not wait to tell people about what I learned and what God had taught me and I could not wait to tell others about it, because God showed me that I could lead people to Christ and with His help I do what I wanted. I got back to work and someone missed at our local store at united furniture in Amory MS, so I had to go to the store and help out and when I got there the manager of the name was James Brown and I not going lie when I heard it I laughed because I thought about the singer, anyway we became good friends and I still see him sometimes at the church I go too. I was moving around furniture and some man came up and ask me about a chair and I sold it to him wrapped it up and put in on the truck by myself and when James came back from the back all he had to do was to take the money and wait on the next person to come in. 2 days later I was at the store for good thank you God, because he was showing me just what he could do in my life if I only believe.

I Saw the Light

This was really the time that I saw the bible at work in my life in alone time, but just because I did not see God at work in my life, that does not mean He was not there, but I was too focused on the world and I what I could get out it to stop and see God working in my life, but this was different, because I was tuned right into God and the plan He had for my life. I thank God He saw through all my mess and still saved my soul when I did not deserve it, because for all the bad I did I really deserved to go to hell, so it shocked me too when God saved my because to tell you the truth I really did not see much worth saving myself but God did, because I'm His child and to me that really sounds good, the child of King, you tell me how does it get better than that? I went around my town and other towns helping people in need and telling about God and now I was at the store I had a computer so I had time to work on my book, so everything God was lining my life up and all had to do was follow.

Ready For TV

I was at the store for about a week and we had all kind of sales going on and I had people coming and buying furniture for everywhere because I know a lot of people and I told them about our good deals, so a lot of them came to check out what we had going on. Larry George the owner would come by and see how things was going and he was not an easily man to please, because he wants everything just right and if you running a business who could blame him, but I did not care this was my chance to prove myself. He told me what to do and I did it and business was so good that Mr. Larry said he wanted to do a commercial and he wanted me in it. I could not believe what I had just heard and I went home and told my wife and kids and they was so happy for me, the next day I got to work there was camera's set up and ready to shoot and I cannot lie I was nervous but with God by my side there was nothing I could not do, so jumped right in and did it.

A Big Star

When I woke up I turned the tv on I saw myself On tv I was blown away, and when I got to the store everyone was talking about it and from that day on, I was big star in Okolona, because we are the little town that does big things. I had so many people coming to the store to meet me and I made sure I sold them something and I tried to tell them about God but I may not have told everyone, because I was really feeling myself and I had good reason too, this was the biggest thing that had ever happen to me and this point in my life was great. I learned no matter what I was doing in my life, God was there and he had my back, but I just want to thank United furniture for giving me the chance to show what I could do and I to thank God for making it all happen anyway.

A New Way of Life

I had people treat me a lot different but that was because they thought I had a lot of money, but really, I was just on tv, but I was on my way. I was doing great in my business life and my personal life was just great, but sometimes I had too much in my personal life and not enough in my home life. I somehow made it all work, but it was not easily, because I was torn between wanting to be single at night but married the next morning. I sometimes did not know what to do, so a lot of times I did what felt right, but after years of long hours away from home it finally caught up with me and when it did it hit me head on. I was not ready for the trouble that came at me but it was my own fault because I was trying to do too many things at one time and at the time I was needed where I was, because me and my wife would not always get alone, but it seem like I always got alone with the women that I was not dating, it was crazy but that was how it was.

Heading to the Mall

There was one time my daughter Doris and her sister and her friend wanted to go to the mall, so when got off work on Saturday, I loaded up and I got my son Mark he was down the road playing basketball with his cousin and we went to the mall in Tupelo. When we got to the mall, I took Mark to the sport shop to buy him some shoes and told the girls to go buy them some clothes and to come get me when they was through so I could pay for the stuff. Mark got some shoes and clothes so he was ready to go, so I look up and there comes Ricketa comes out of the store with a bad look on her face and I ask her what was wrong and she said that I was not going to like it and went into the store and the bill was almost $300 dollars and I just came in and paid it with no problem. I was making $1000 a week and I had $1500 in my pocket so I did not care what it cost as long as my family was happy, and I just wanted to let them know that I was there no matter what. The kids in my life made me step up and be a man because for once I had somebody that was counting on me, and I was not going to let them down.

Time to Move On

I was making a lot of money with my glass plaque, and what I would do was write you a poem using a little of what you would tell me about how you felt about your loved one, or for Mother`s day and Valentine day, it was going great. I had 2 jobs and I was taking advantages of being on tv to further my career in writing, because God promised me one day I would have my books in stores , and I told God if I could have my book at one store I would be happy, but God gave me that and a whole lot more. My book is in about 10 stores in Okolona and in Barnes and noble which is worldwide so I can only thank God for that. The main thing I learned from this was when you don't see God's hands in your life, that is when God was fighting the hardest to save your life, but how can someone help you if don't believe in them in the first place. How can you blame God for what is wrong in your life and then tell people you don't believe in God, my friend you cannot have it both ways, so pick a side and stick with it.

A New Time in Life

I was amazed at what God did in my life, and sometimes people could not believe that I could write such wonderful things down but what they did not realize this gift did not come from me but from God. I not going to say I had the best life or the best things in life but at least I'm saved and I guess that is more than I can say for some, so thank God for that. There is a lot of stories in my life but for time sake I'm going to give you the highlights. I started writing a lot more and helping a lot more people out and God has blessed me more and more, so that is one reason I kept doing it because I was helping people and it made me feel good inside. I worked hard at United to make sure my job was done right, but I also had my side business going on, so my life was going great. The thing about it was everything I was doing was amazing everyone else but the one person that was really amazed was me, because I never knew I could do anything close to this, but with God on my side I cannot fell.

What Is Most Important

I found out quick in my life what was important in my life, because at the end of the day my family was all I had and told myself that one day I going to make them proud of me, because some people cannot look past the old me to see the new me, but I'm not really doing it for them anyway, it is really all for God. There is one reason I say what I say because God is the one who in control of everything, and He is the one that can make things happen so that is the reason I will always stick by God.

God Saved Granny

My grandmother had a hole in her heart one day and then after some time God healed her and close the hole in her heart. There have been a lot of times that God healed my grandmother, when I was little my grandmother told about God and His love, and this we saw it firsthand. In my life, I have come to realize there is no love like the love of the Lord. The doctors didn't know what do, because she was too old to do surgery so really there was nothing the doctors could do but let her use up what was left of her bad heart, and then something amazing happen my Grandmother ask God to fix her broken old heart with a hole in it and He did. My Grandmother went to her doctor to talk about her bad heart, so the doctor ran some test on her heart and the test showed that there was no hole in her heart, and my Grandmother stopped right then and thanked the Lord.

Chapter 15

How Good God Has Been

Thanks to God, I was able to travel around some of this great big world, and I will go anywhere that God sends me. I found out a lot of things by doing all this traveling but one thing I found out that was it don`t matter how bad you think you have it there is a lot of people that has it worse. I remember being in Washington Dc and going my hotel and complaining that it was not as good as some, and the people living on the streets. I think if more people would focus on God and not on what they got or what they don`t got they would be better off. I still mess up every day, in one form or another but I also try help people out but that is not good enough for some people, but that is the reason why I`m glad they are not my judge and it is Lord above.

Gone to the Picnic

I remember it was like yesterday me and my friend James Hill and his wife went to a picnic and it was sponsored by united furniture, so we all loaded up in my car and we went. They had all kind of rides for the kids, and they even had face painting, but thing I loved was riding the big tricycle in the mud and falling down everyone was laughing but despite me our team still won and got get into the money machine but that was harder than it looks. I caught back up with Hill and his wife and I said I was going to take a picture by myself as I look up there is this beautiful lady in front of me and she ask if could take a picture with me and we took a picture together and at that moment we had instant chemistry. I went and got her name she said it Linda Gates and she hung out and talked the rest of the day. I was not sure what it was but there was something special about this woman that was drawing me to her.

Could Be Love

I called her up and ask to come hang we really didn't do much but enjoy each other company, hung out talked about who each other was and who she was kin to, and to find out I knew her whole family most of my life, like they say it a small world after all. I knew by hanging out with her that I didn't want be apart from her, but at the same time she was kindly in a relationship but by her spending time with me that was about to end, because believe me when I need to my game is tight. I use to run game on women the same way the run game on me, but for the time in a long time I don't have to run game but be myself, and see she was feeling me too. I started picking her up at work and sometimes she would spend the night, but after 2 months of back and forth from Aberdeen to Okolona, we decided for Linda to move in and we have been together ever since, and there has been some good times and bad, but one thing we have each other back and we love each other very much and one day very soon if she still we have me, will be my wife, because I love her very much.

My Family Tree

My family tree is so crazy, but I guess it takes all kinds of different people to make up a family, and my family is no exceptions. I love my family and there nothing I would not do for them and all I want is to show them I'm not the same person, now I'm the one everyone can count on. I going try to be there for my family and other people, but with everything going on it in this world it is impossible to help everyone but I challenge everyone who is reading this to see if you can help someone out, you never know what difference you can make until you try. People will say there is nothing good about me and if that is the way they think, I can't do nothing about that, but one thing I can do is tell them I sorry, and if they don't expect it that is not on me anymore, but the one thing you can do like me is follow the Lord and He will take care of the rest.

Can't Kill the Hoss

There is a lot that God did for me and I didn't even know it at first but after I got grown I saw that there a lot of times I should have been died but God saved me, and my family. Mother told me I was born in a toilet, she said she went to use the bathroom and I came out, I found out why I like to swim so much, and all my mother had to do was flush and I would be clean. When I was young fell in a deep hole and was not hurt, I have be beaten with hoes, bullwhips, belts, sticks, and stomped down until I thought I was dead, but God kept picking me back up and I left coming back for more. I know some of you would say why didn't you just stay down, but I had my sisters depending on me, so no matter what I had to keep them safe.

Thank God for Everything

I want to thank God for everything He did in my life and in my family's life. I like to thank my mom which I will always love, and my grandmother for always sticking by me and for putting God in my heart when I didn't even know Him. I want to say thank you to Juanita and David for really saving my life because if it was not for them, I really believe I would have been dead or in prison. I would like to tell my sisters that I love all of you. I would like to tell my brother Roger that I love him too, and with us if one swing both swing no matter what. I try to show my brother how to talk and no fight but somethings it's hard. I want to thank my baby Linda Gates for sticking by me all the years don't worry one day we will get it right. There are too many names to name but to the ones that done helped me on my way thank you.

The End

This is the end of this book, but not the end of my life, so there are more books to come. I may not do much in this life but the one thing I can do is serve the Lord and write my books because I have to tell people about the Lord and what he did in my life. I see God at work all the time in my life and around me but first you must know the difference between God`s voice and the devils and a lot of times I knew it was God`s but still I did not do right, so what does that say about me but like I said, all I do is say I sorry and I will try to do better and that is all God ask of any of us. In closing always be faithful to God, and always love your family because you never know how long they will be here, and always following your dreams and just like me one day they your dreams will come true.

Special Thanks

I would like to first thank God because He is the head of my life, and without Him none of this would be possible. The main reason I was cutting up so bad when I was young was I miss my mom and felt like no one loved me so I acted out, because the reason I wrote was not to put you down, it was to show you what I had do to get back to you. I want to thank you for just being my Mother, and no matter what happens in life I will always love you. To Linda Gates thank you for seeing past our differences and giving me a chance and for having my back, and I know I may not show it all the time but I really love you and I really can't wait to make you my wife. I want to tell my brother Roger Denton that I love him, I would not tell him to his face because he probably would punch me in the face, but that is my brother and I love him. When we were young, we didn't get to spend time together but we were young and was nothing I could do about it but we our together, because you are not just my brother but my best friend.

Special Thanks Part 2

I want to thank Juanita and David for adopting me, when I made it hard for anybody to love, but both you made me part of your family thank you. David thank you for not only being a Dad when I needed it, but you was my friend because some of the things we did or talked about or the millions of times you bailed me out of things, but I'm truly sorry for all the hell I caused you, but now I vow if it is the last I do I going make you proud of me. Juanice I love you so much and I'm so proud to call you my sister, I just remember when you to go dog catching with us and me and Dad had to run after the dogs and you would just call them and they would just come up to you, them was good times and I love you very much. Carolyn and Cindy, you two are my heart and my soul and I would give my life for either one of you, words cannot say how much I love you too. I would also tell my youngest sister Caitlyn that even know I may not have talked about you a lot, that does not mean I don't love you, if you need me I will be there because I'm still your big brother, so proud of you sis.

Special Thanks Part 3

I would like to thank my Grandmother for always sticking by and loving me, and for showing me God when I didn't know He was there. I would like to give thanks to my road dog buck, we had been up and down the road together, we have outrun, out drank, and shut down just about every party we went to. Buck is the one man if he said something that is what he meant, if I ever need him, he will there and it's the same with me. I also want to give thanks to Water boy you are the friend everyone would like to have because he will always be there when you need him. I want to say thank you Ricketa, and Doris and Mark for letting feels what is like to be a real dad, even though you are not my real kids, in my heart it is real as it gets and you and your kids very much. I want to dedicate this book to my son Samuel Steven Jordan Edwards; daddy will always love you and one day I will be in heaven with you. I want to thank Nicole Mangum for Publishing my book and being my friend and traveling around with me and telling people about Christ, God bless everyone that believes in God, please don't give up on Him.

Pray and Get Out of the Way

My family it was time for me to leave this place on earth, and go see God and get a rebirth, so don't sit around with all that crying, and a lot of people lying about how they was going to miss me the most, but never came to visit me it must be a hoax. So, family if you want to do one final thing for me, it would be to live your life free, free of all the stress and all the mess of putting someone down like you got a crown on your head, but really if was not for God we all would have been dead. It's time for me to pass on but all of you are still here, but just like me you never knew your last breath could be near. I learned one thing in life that took me a long way, pray and get out of the way, and things are not always going to go your way that is the reason I say pray and get out the way. My family I'm not dead, but I just went ahead, but if you are saved I will see you again, but don't be like my other friends, doomed in hell for listening to the lies the devil had to tell. Keep God in your heart and never stray away and I will see you again someday.

From WILLIE BOGAN to my family, do not let the love for our family die with me, I love all of you very much and I hope my death will bring my family closer, so remember this is not goodbye, it's so long for now but I will see you later.